CHINA'S GRADUATE EDUCATION QUALITY-DATA ON FIVE ASPECTS 2017

5说中国研究生教育质量 2017

王战军／主编
Wang Zhanjun / Chief Editor

『数』说研究生教育质量
『事』说研究生教育质量
『省』说研究生教育质量
『生』说研究生教育质量
『他』说研究生教育质量

Data on Graduate Education Quality
Events about Graduate Education Quality
Graduate Education Quality in Each Province
Graduate Education Quality from Students' Perspective
International Reviews of Graduate Education

科学普及出版社
·北 京·

图书在版编目（CIP）数据

五说中国研究生教育质量：2017=CHINA'S GRADUATE EDUCATION QUALITY DATE ON FIVE ASPECTS：2017：汉、英 / 王战军主编 .—北京：科学普及出版社，2017. 8

ISBN 978-7-110-09652-9

Ⅰ. ①五… Ⅱ. ①王… Ⅲ. ①研究生教育—教育质量—研究报告—中国—2017—汉、英 Ⅳ. ① G643

中国版本图书馆 CIP 数据核字（2017）第 190768 号

策划编辑	王晓义
责任编辑	王晓义　蒋宵宵
装帧设计	中文天地
责任校对	焦　宁
责任印制	徐　飞

出　　版	科学普及出版社
发　　行	中国科学技术出版社发行部
地　　址	北京市海淀区中关村南大街16号
邮　　编	100081
发行电话	010-62173865
传　　真	010-62179148
网　　址	http://www.cspbooks.com.cn

开　　本	850mm × 1168mm　1/32
字　　数	60千字
印　　张	2.5
版　　次	2017年8月第1版
印　　次	2017年8月第1次印刷
印　　刷	北京盛通印刷股份有限公司
书　　号	ISBN 978-7-110-09652-9 / G · 4047
定　　价	24.00元

编 委 会

Editorial Committee

前言

2016 年是“十三五”开局之年，我国研究生教育持续深化综合改革，唱响研究生教育“强体”“提质”的强音。

加强质量评价，优化研究生教育结构。2016 年国务院学位委员会对全国 205 个学位授予单位完成了学位授权点动态调整，共撤销授权点 576 个，增列 367 个。公布了 2014 年学位授权点专项

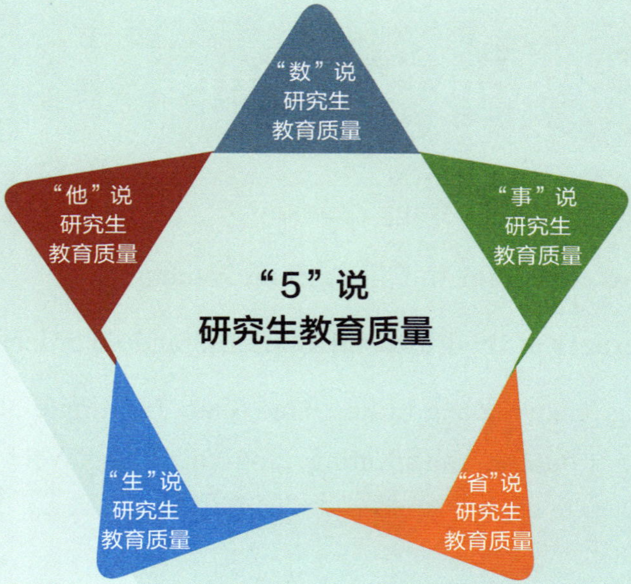

Preface

2016 was the first year of China's 13th Five-Year Plan. In this year, China continued to deepen the comprehensive reform of the graduate education, by setting the strong tone emphasizing the graduate education should be further in "reinforced mechanism" and "quality improvement".

Strengthen the quality evaluation and optimize the structure of graduate education. In 2016, the Academic Degrees Committee of the State Council completed the national dynamic adjustment of the degree authorization units totaling 205, with annuling 576 units and adding 367 units, hence the structure of the graduate education system was further

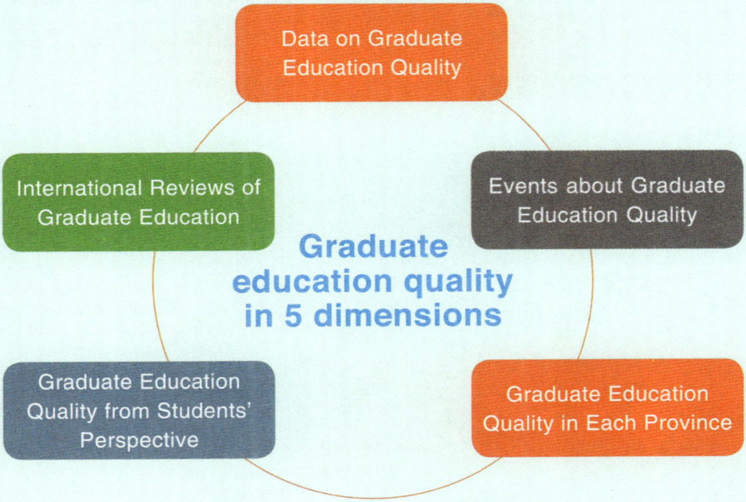

评估结果，撤销了50个“不合格”授权点，对95个“限期整改”授权点给予暂停招生、限期整改处理。全面开展MBA教育自查自纠与专项整治，并对全日制和非全日制研究生做出明确界定，规范招生、投入、就业等要求，加强了研究生教育培养质量评价。

以“服务需求、提高质量”为主线，深化培养模式改革。研究生培养单位的人才培养定位于主动服务国家对外开放战略，对接“一带一路”等国家重大战略。与此同时，研究生培养单位也在加强结构调整优化和培养模式转变，构建良好学术生态环境，凸显办学特色。

专业学位研究生教育综合改革多举并用。2016年，教育部要求统一组织实施全日制和非全日制研究生招生录取，坚持全日制和非全日制研究生教育同一质量标准；搭建专业学位案例库公共平台，建立了多部门参与的专业学位研究生联合培养体系，建设了多个专业学位教学案例库。

optimized. It announced the results of the specific assessment of the degree granting units, which was carried out in 2014. 50 "unqualified" authorization units were revoked, 95 degree granting units facing "rectification deadline", which were suspended the enrollment of students, and requested a rectification with limited time. The whole measures effectively promoted the graduate training units to improve their graduate education quality continuously. The government comprehensively implemented the self-examination and self-correction and specific rectification of MBA education and made a clear definition of the full-time and part-time graduate students, specified the requirements of the enrollment, investment, employment and so on, which had strengthened the quality evaluation of the graduate education training.

Hold the main line of "serving needs and improving quality" and deepen the training model reform. Graduate education training units should initiatively aim at serving the country's strategy of "opening up", "Belt and Road Initiative" etc. Meanwhile, the units should strengthen the structural adjustment and optimization and the training mode transform, to build an excellent academic ecological environment and highlight its academic characteristics.

A number of initiatives had been enabled in the comprehensive reform of professional degree graduate education. In 2016, the Ministry of Education requested a unified organization and implementation in the enrollment of full-time and part-time graduate students, adhering to the same quality standards for the two types of graduate education. The public case database of professional degree programs was set up, a joint training system with multi-sectoral collaboration for the professional degree graduation was established and a number of case databases for professional degree teaching and learning were built.

目 录

Contents

目 录

Contents

Graduate Education Quality from Students' Perspective

International Reviews of Graduate Education

一、“数”说 研究生教育质量

（一）研究生教育质量，你必须知道的“7个数”

1. 培养单位数

2016年，全国共有研究生培养单位793个。

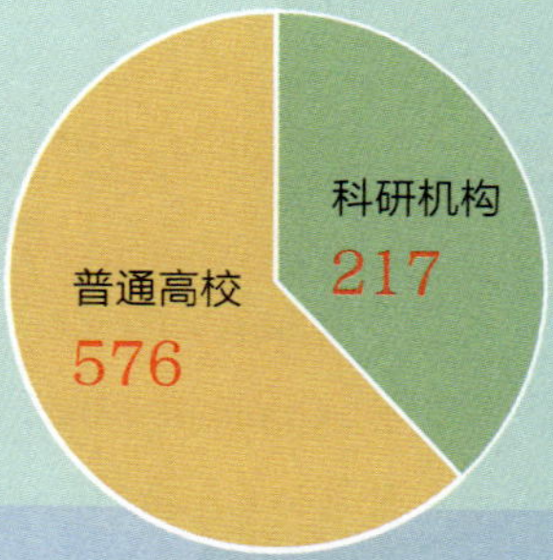

2. 在校研究生数

2016年，我国在学研究生总人数达2,585,605人。其中，在校研究生共计1,981,051人，在职人员攻读研究生学位581,843人，研究生课程进修班22,711人。

Data on Graduate Education Quality

I. 7 types of data on graduate education quality

1. Data on institutions

In 2016, the number of institutions offering graduate education has reached 793.

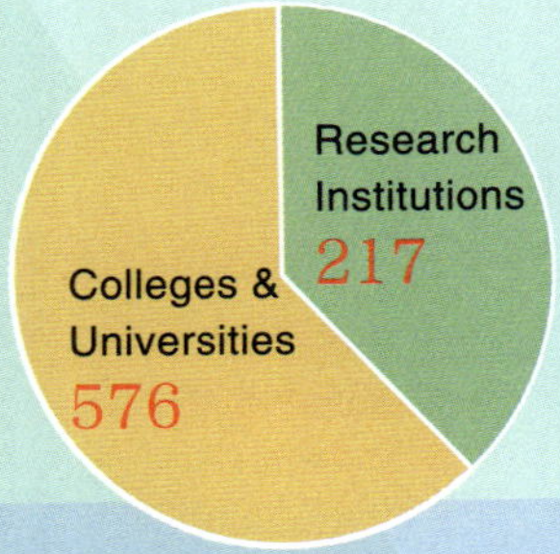

2. Data on the amount of graduate students

In 2016, the overall number of graduate students in China reached 2,585,605, including 1,981,051 full-time graduate students, 581,843 part-time graduate students and 22,711 students taking graduate courses.

3. 研招人数

（1）2016 年共招收研究生 667,064 人。其中，博士研究生 77,252 人，硕士研究生 589,812 人。

（2）硕士研究生招生：学术学位硕士研究生 309,990 人，专业学位硕士研究生 279,822 人。

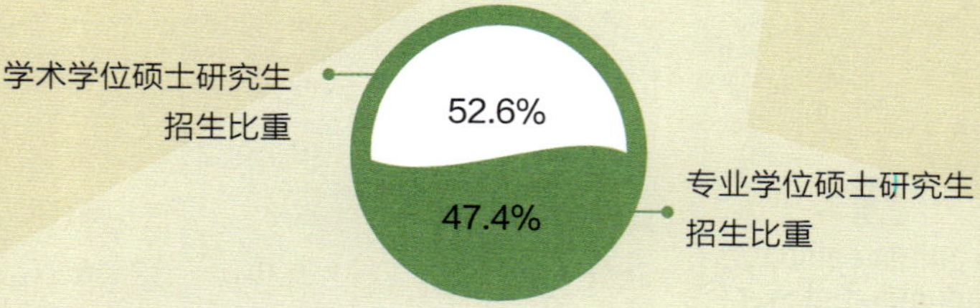

（3）从学科来看，招收人数最多的是工学，共 232,414 人，占比 34.86%（图 1.1）。

3. Data on enrollments of graduate students

A. The total number of enrollments in 2016 was 667,064, with 77,252 Ph.D. candidates and 589,812 master's degree candidates.

B. As for the enrollment scale of master's degree students, the number of academic degree students and professional degree students were 309,990 and 279,822 respectively.

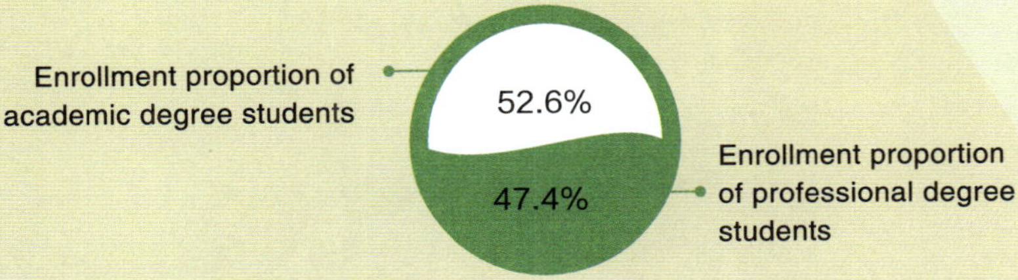

C. Compared with other disciplines, engineering got the largest enrollment scale with 232,414 students and accounted for 34.86% of all (Chart 1.1).

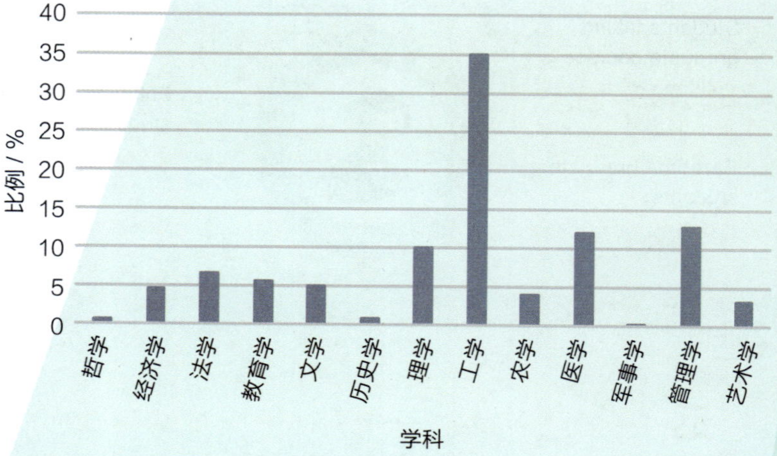

图 1.1 2016 年分学科研究生招生比例

4. 毕业生数

（1）2016 年共毕业研究生 563,938 人，博士毕业生 55,011 人，硕士毕业生 508,927 人。

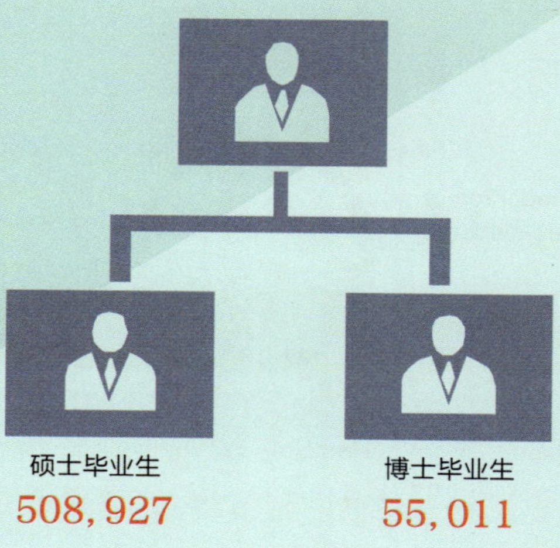

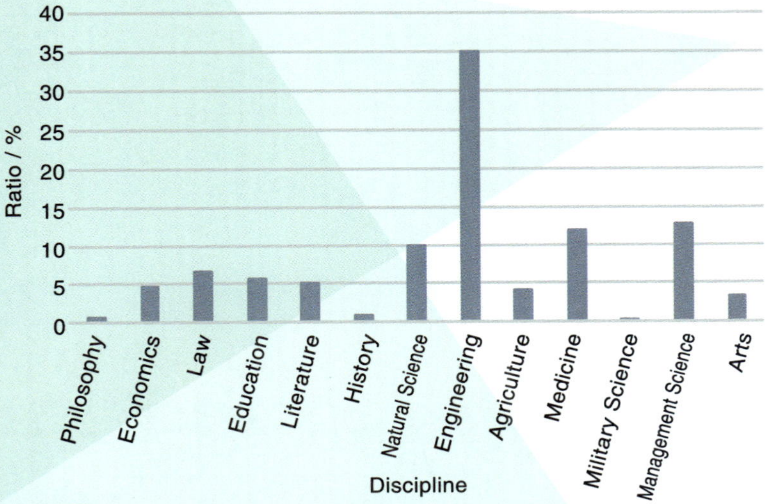

Chart 1.1 The proportion of graduate students enrollment by discipline in 2016.

4. Data on graduates

A. In 2016, there were 563,938 students accomplished their graduate education, with 55,011 got Ph.Ds and 508,927 got master's degrees.

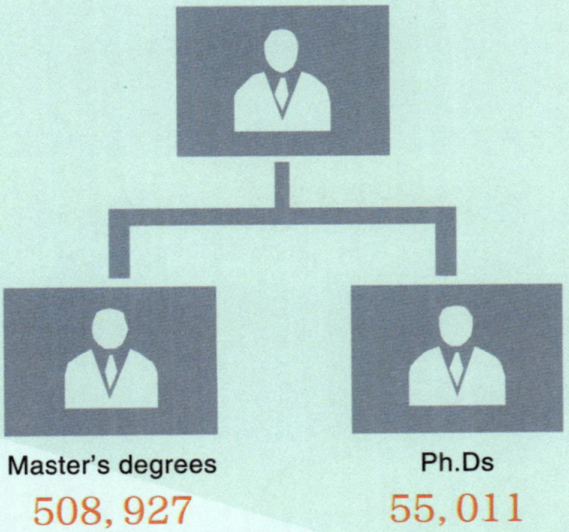

（2）毕业人数最多的是工学毕业生，有近 20 万人（图 1.2）。

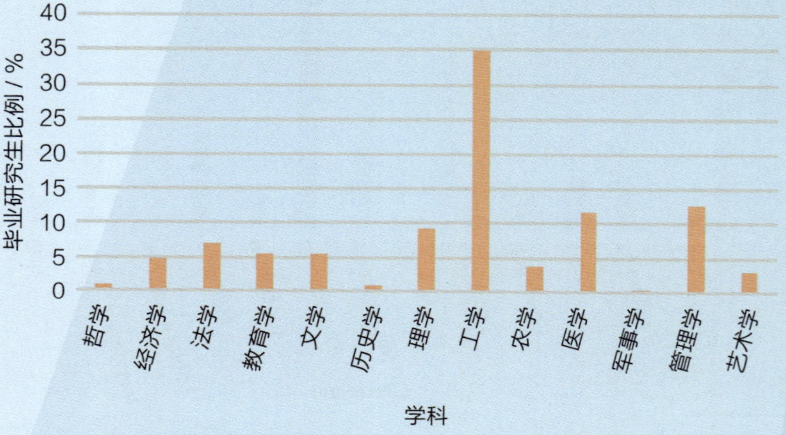

图 1.2　2016 年各学科研究生毕业比例

5. 来华留学生研究生数

2016 年来华攻读研究生学位的有 63,867 人，同比增加 19.22%。

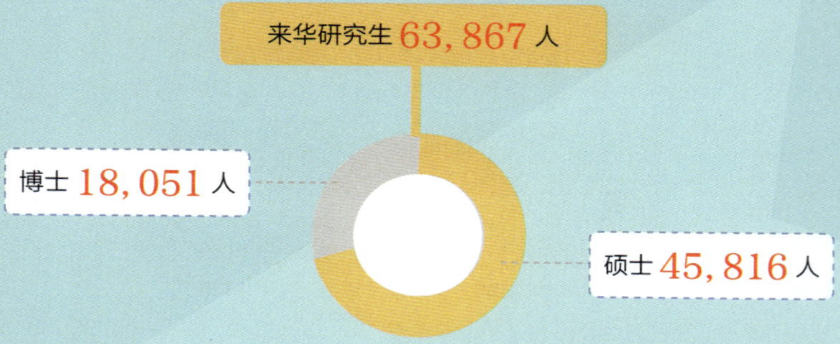

B. Engineering was the discipline with largest number of graduates, almost 200,000 (Chart 1.2).

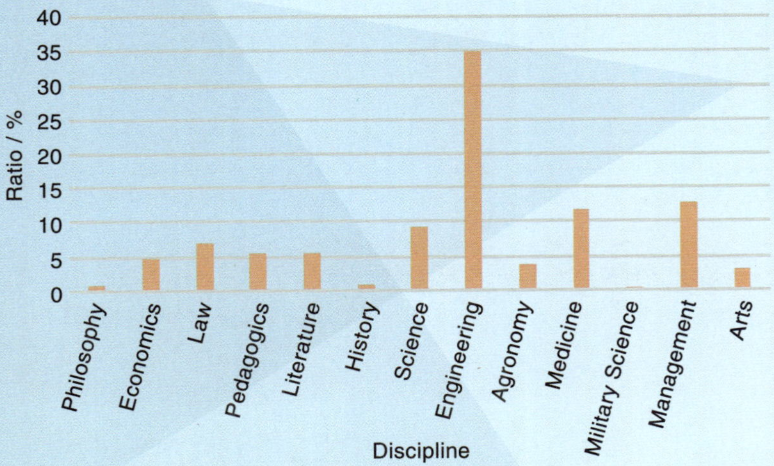

Chart 1.2 Graduation proportion by discipline in 2016

5. Data on international graduate students

In 2016, the number of international graduate students reached 63,867, increased 19.22% compared with 2015.

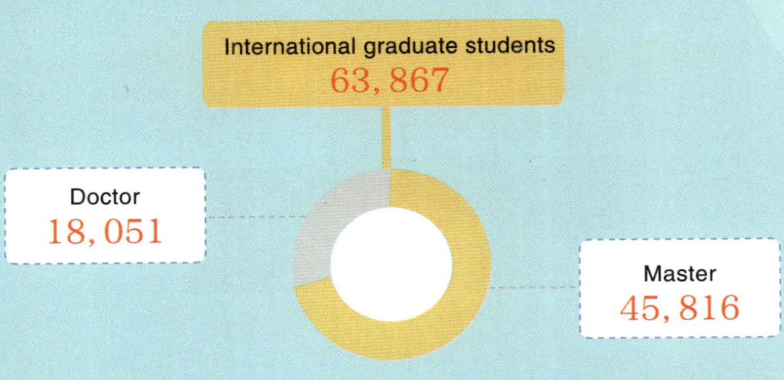

6. 教育经费投入数

2015 年，全国教育经费总投入为 36,129.19 亿元，同比增长 10.13%。

2015 年，高校生均公共财政预算教育事业费排在前三名的地区分别是北京市、西藏自治区和上海市。

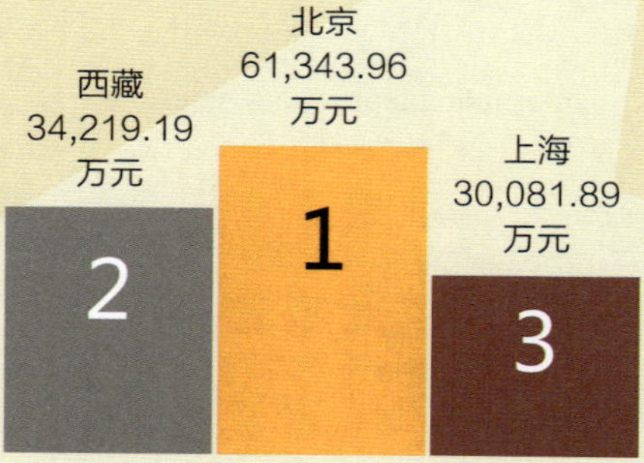

6. Data on educational funds investment

In 2015, the total investment in education was 3,612,919 million yuan, with a year-on-year growth by 10.13%.

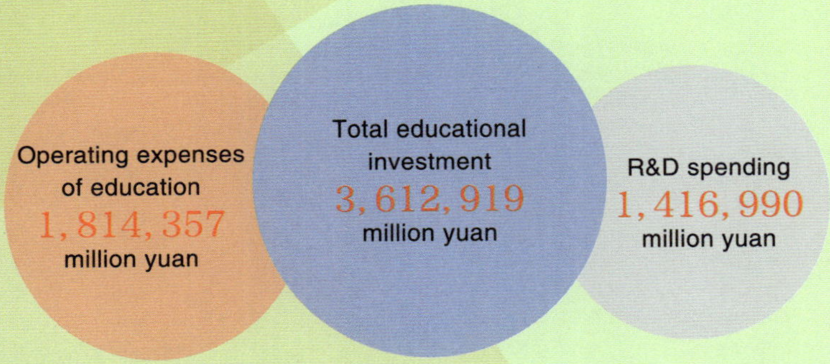

In 2015, the top three provinces/municipalities on the students' average budget expenditure in higher education are Beijing, Tibet and Shanghai.

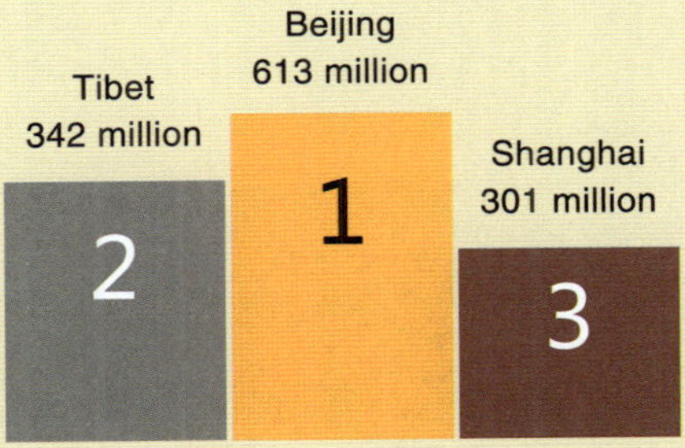

7. 奖／助学金数

2016年，研究生国家奖学金共计奖励研究生**4.5万**人，研究生学业奖学金共奖励研究生**132.18万**人，研究生“三助”岗位津贴共资助**164.93万**人次。

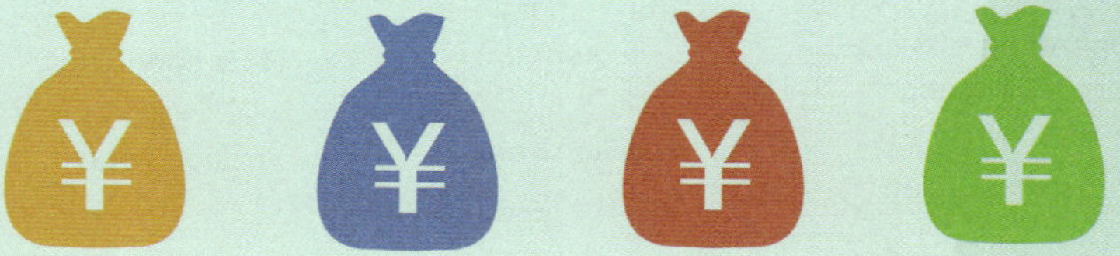

国家奖学金 10亿元

学业奖学金 93.25亿元

国家助学金 109.93亿元

“三助”岗位津贴 45.39亿元

7. Data on scholarship and financial aid

In 2016, the national scholarship, the academic scholarship and the national financial aid for graduate students helped 45,000, 1,321,800 and 1,649,300 students, respectively.

National scholarship 1,000 million yuan

Academic scholarship 9,325million yuan

National financial aid 10,993million yuan

Three-assistance allowance 4,539 million yuan

（二）大数据告诉你 2016 年研究生教育质量“杠不杠”

1. 研究生招生数“加速行驶”

2009—2016 年，研究生招生规模年均增长率为 **3.88%**，特点是稳中有增。增长的招生规模 90% 以上用于招收硕士研究生（图 1.3 和图 1.4）。

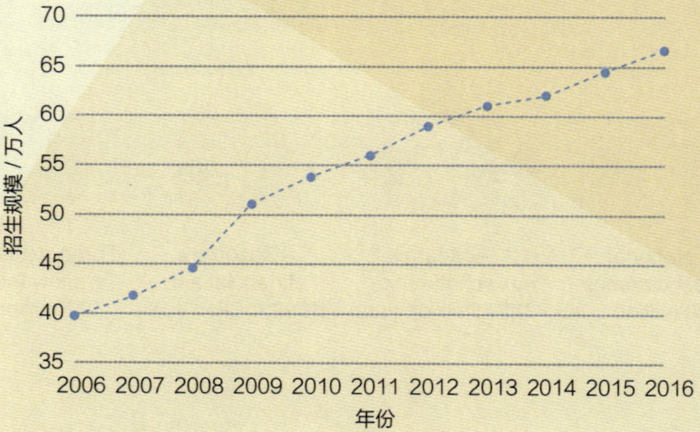

图 1.3　2006—2016 年研究生招生情况

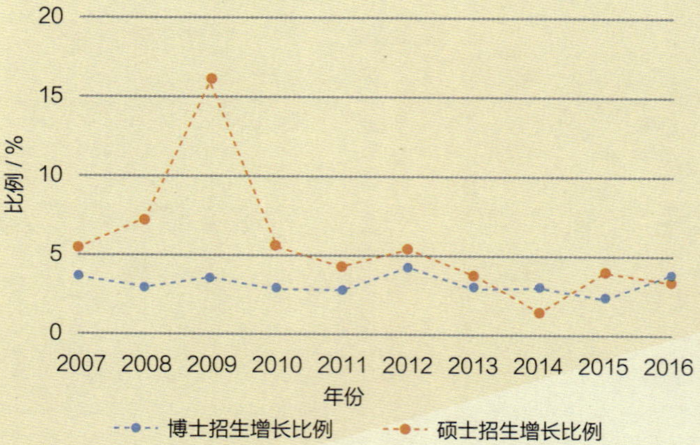

图 1.4　2006—2016 年博士研究生、硕士研究生招生增长比例

II. Big data on graduate education quality in 2016

1. The enrollment number increased steadily

The average annual growth rate of enrollment for graduate students was **3.88%** from 2009 to 2016. The enrollment number shows a steady growth, and over 90% of the growth came from master's enrollment (Chart 1.3 & Chart 1.4).

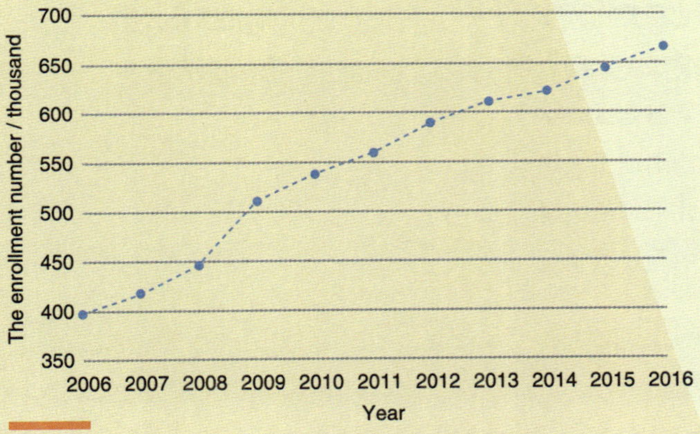

Chart 1.3 The enrollment condition during 2006-2016

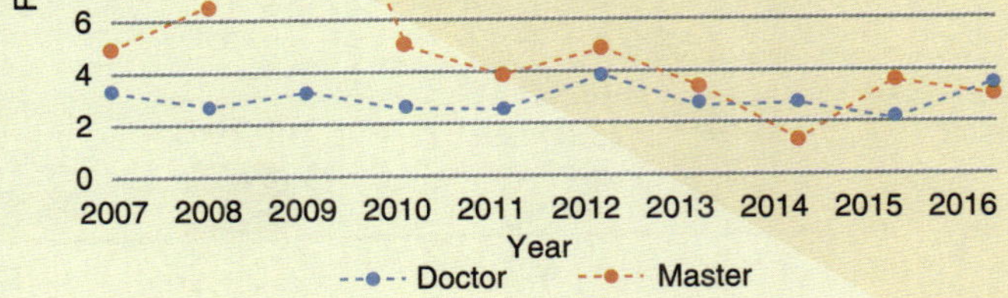

Chart 1.4 Growth rate of graduate students' enrollment during 2006-2016

2. 研究生就业状况“春光灿烂”

（1）33 所有研究生总体就业率数据的高校中，25 所研究生就业率超过 95%。

研究生就业率≥ 99% 的高校 6 所

北京交通大学
北京中医药大学
华东理工大学
华南理工大学
北京邮电大学
中国戏剧学院

研究生就业率 <90% 的高校 2 所

东北林业大学
陕西师范大学

（2）50 所有硕士研究生就业率数据的高校中，43 所高校的硕士研究生就业率超过 95%。

硕士研究生就业率≥ 99% 的高校占比为 28%（14 所）。

硕士研究生就业率 <90% 的高校占比为 4%（2 所）。

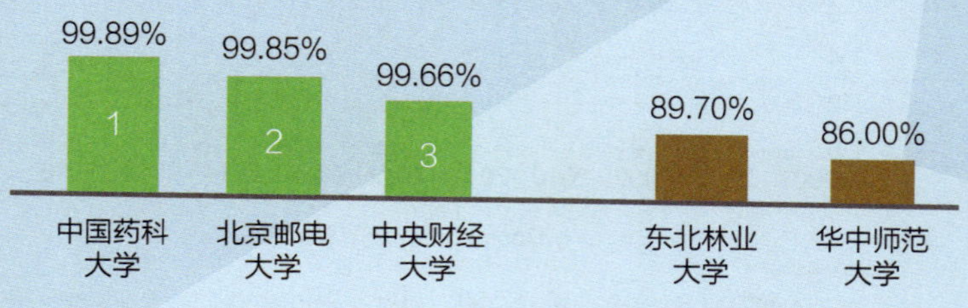

2. Employment situation is quite well

A. 25 universities' graduate employment rate was over 95%, among the 33 universities who performed well in graduate employment.

6 universities' graduate employment rate ≥99%

Beijing Jiaotong University
Beijing University of Chinese Medicine
East China University of Science and Technology
South China University of Technology
Beijing University of Posts and Telecommunications
National Academy of Chinese Theater Arts

2 universities' graduate employment rate <90%

Northeast Forestry University
Shaanxi Normal University

B. 43 universities' master's graduate employment rate was over 95%, among the 50 universities who behaved well in graduate employment.

Universities with employment rate of master's graduate students ≥99%, accounting for 28% (14).

Universities with employment rate of master's graduate students <90%, accounting for 4% (2).

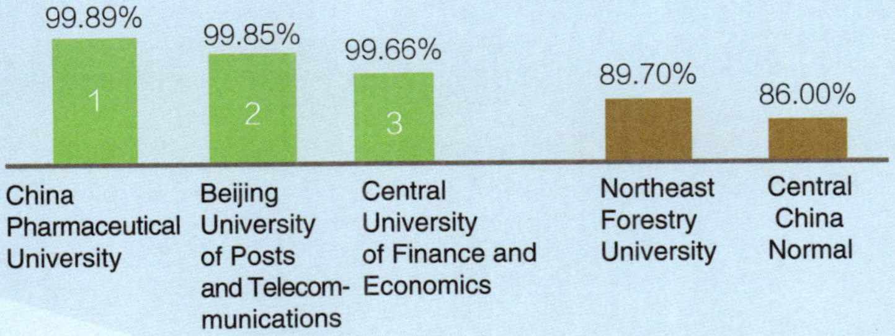

（3）49 所有**博士研究生就业率**数据的高校中，39 所高校的硕士研究生就业率超过 95%。

博士研究生就业率 ≥ 99% 的高校占比 26.5%（13 所），其中：

北京邮电大学　　中央音乐学院　　合肥工业大学

博士研究生就业率达 100%

博士研究生就业率 <90% 的高校有 3 所，占比 6.1%（3 所），其中：

东北林业大学	华中农业大学	中山大学
83.48%	86.31%	88.63%

3. 研究生参与科技创新人数“小蹦一下”

2016 年，研究生参加当年获得资助的国家自然科学基金累计 137,270 人次。

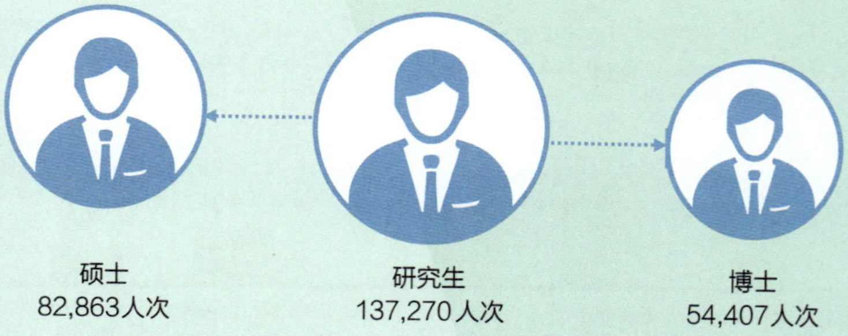

C. Among **49** universities which had the data of employment rate of doctor graduate students, **39** universities passed **95%**.

Universities with employment rate of doctor graduate students ≥**99%**, accounting for **26.5%** (**13**), and 3 universities are outstanding.

Beijing University of Posts and Telecommunication	Central Conservatory of Music	Hefei University of Technology

Employment rate of doctor graduate students reached100%

Universities with employment rate of doctor graduate students **<90%**, accounting for 6.1% (**3**):

Northeast Forestry University	Huazhong Agricultural University	Sun Yat-sen University
83.48%	86.31%	88.63%

3. The amount of graduate students participating in scientific innovations increased slightly

The number of graduate students participating in funding natural science foundation of China had added up to **137,270** in 2016.

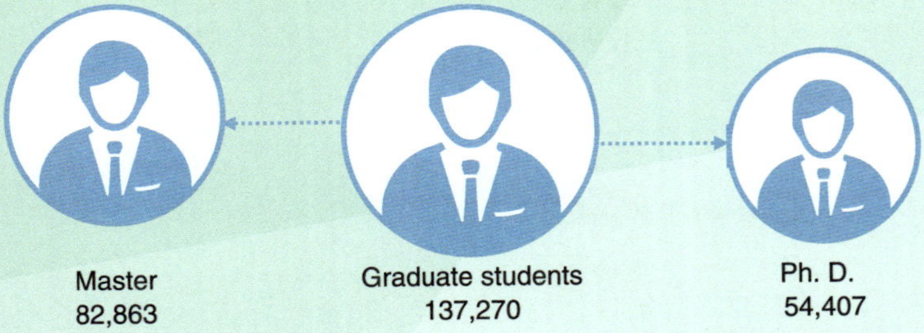

4. 研究生导师数“爆发洪荒之力”

研究生指导教师从 2007 年的 206,034 人增长到 2016 年的 378,947 人，增长了 **83.92%**（图 1.5）。

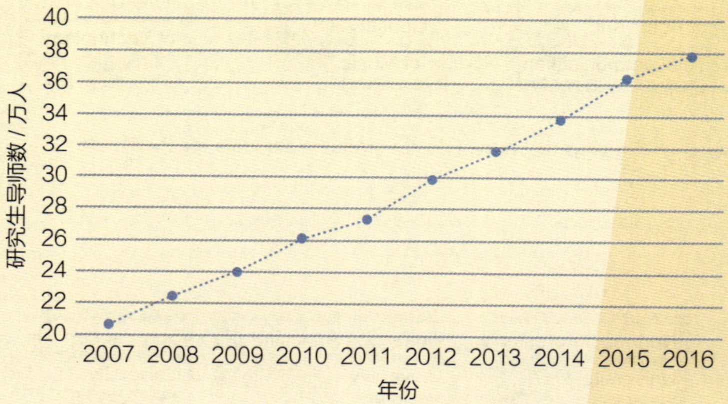

图 1.5　2007—2016 年我国研究生导师数

研究生指导教师的增幅大大超过在校研究生的增幅。

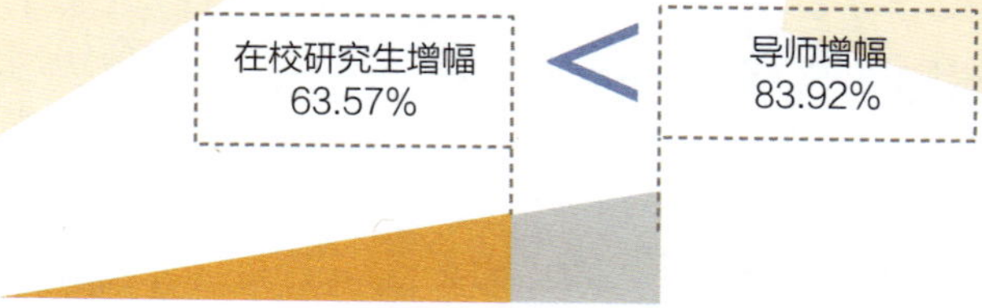

4. The number of graduate supervisors increased rapidly

The population of graduate supervisors increased from 206,034 in 2007 to 378,947 in 2016, with a growth rate of 83.92% (Chart 1.5).

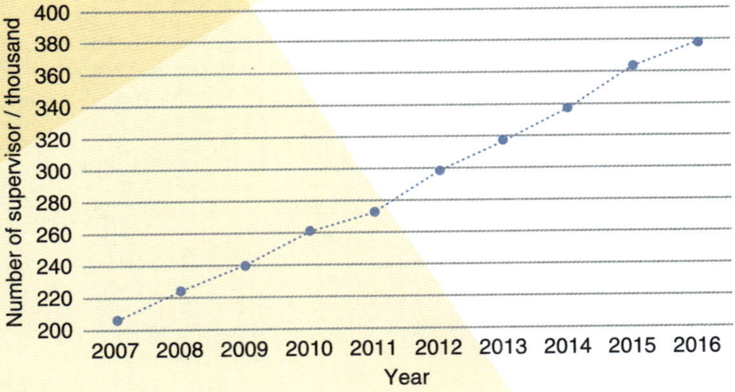

Chart 1.5 The amount of graduate supervisors, 2007-2016

Growth rate of graduate supervisors exceeds that of postgraduate students.

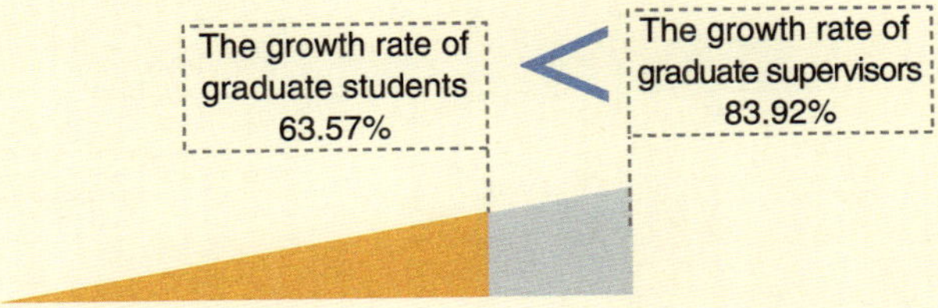

5. 专业学位研究生招生数“火力全开”

2016 年在校专业学位研究生是 2009 年的 **5.7** 倍（图 1.6）。

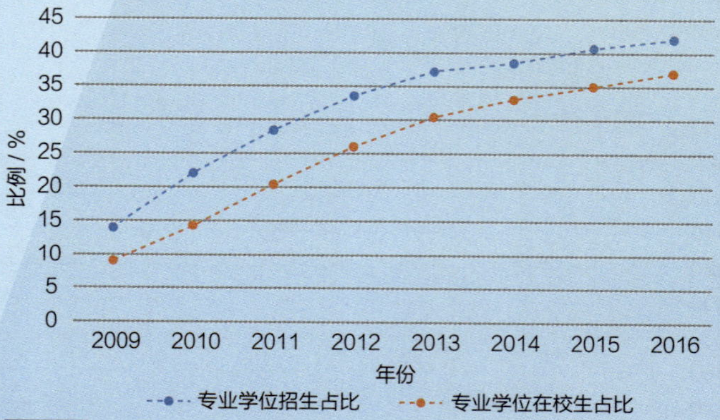

图 1.6　2009—2016 年专业学位学生招生比例

6. 来华留学研究生人数“要上天”

2009—2016 年，来华留学的**博士**研究生从 **4,751** 人增长到 **18,051** 人，硕士研究生从 **14,227** 人增长到 **45,816** 人（图 1.7）。

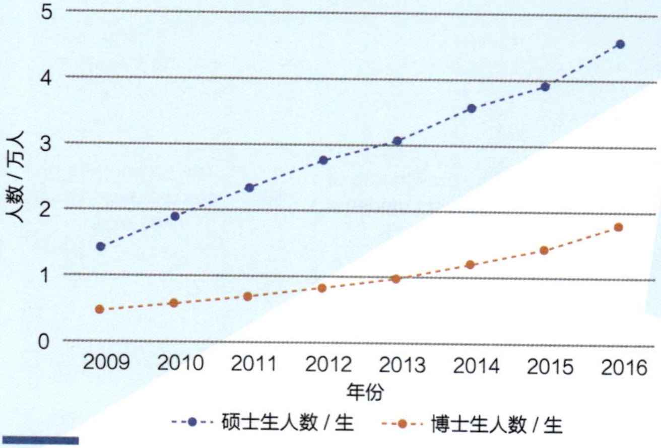

图 1.7　2009—2016 年来华攻读研究生学位人数

5. Continuous increase of professional degree enrollment rate

The number of professional degree students on campus in 2016 was 5.7 times that in 2009 (Chart 1.6).

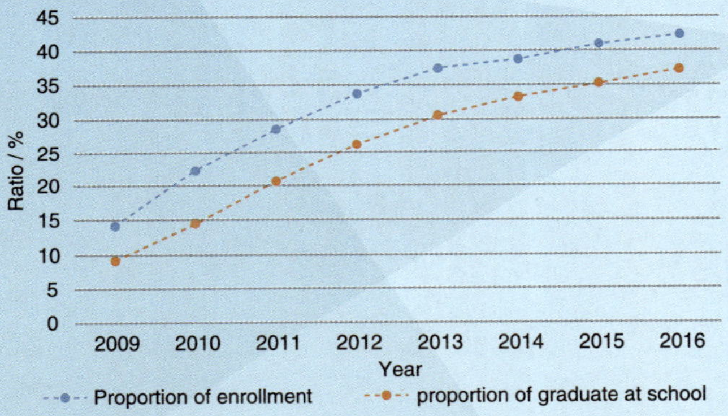

Chart 1.6 Proportion of the enrollment and graduates of professional students from 2009 to 2016

6. The population of international graduate students grew tremendously

From 2009 to 2016, the number of international students pursuing doctorate degree increased from 4,751 to 18,051. And the amount of international students pursuing master's degree increased from 14,227 to 45,816 (Chart 1.7).

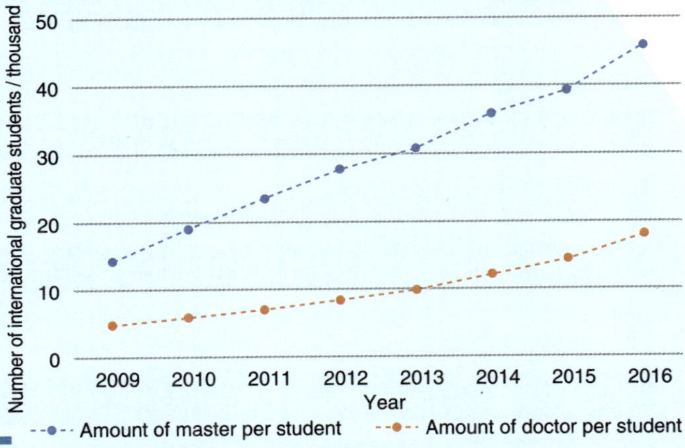

Chart 1.7 The increase of the international graduate students in China for graduate education from 2009 to 2016

二、“事”说 研究生教育质量

（一）2016 年度不容错过的研究生教育质量十大事件

1. 国家学位管理最高机构召开会议，聚焦研究生教育质量发展
2. 教育部统筹管理全日制和非全日制研究生，坚持同一质量标准发展
3. 国家加强学位授权点专项评估，动态调整学位授权点
4. 国家“双一流”战略政策引领建设一流研究生教育体系
5. 中国学位与研究生教育学会创设多个奖项促进研究生教育发展
6. 南京大学启动“二三三”硕士研究生教育改革
7. 西安交通大学开展专业学位研究生教育“供给侧改革”
8. 国内研究生培养单位首设研究生教育学博士硕士学科专业
9. 高度重视研究生教育过程管理，杜绝恶性事件发生
10. 依法治教：北京法院审理首例考研替考入刑案

Events about Graduate Education Quality

I. 10 hot issues regarding graduate education quality in 2016

1. Meeting held by the highest-level committee of National Degree Management, focusing on graduate education quality improvement
2. Ministry of Education coordinating on the full-time and part-time graduate education with equivalent quality standard
3. The Government enhancing the thematic evaluation of the degree authorization units and adjusting the degree authorization units dynamically
4. Decision made to build first-class graduate education under the guidance of the "Double First-rate" strategy
5. Chinese Society of Academic Degrees and Graduate Education establishing awards to promote the development of graduate education
6. Nanjing University initiating '2-3-3' reform for master's education
7. Xi'an Jiaotong University launching 'Supply-side Structural Reform' of professional degree education
8. First programs on graduate education for master's degree and PhD established in China
9. Decision made to pay high attention to process management of graduate education to eliminate malignant events
10. Decision made to manage education by law: Beijing Court hearing the first criminal case of surrogate exam-taker for graduate entrance examination

（二）面对“研究生教育”，清华 & 苏州大学怎么做

1. 清华大学研究生教育

2016 年清华大学研究生教育改革主要举措：

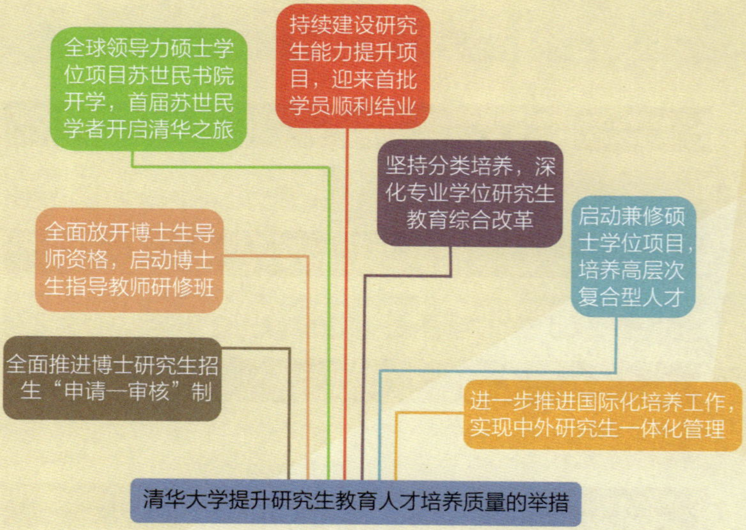

II. Tsinghua & Soochow Universities' Efforts to Promote Graduate Education

1. Graduate education in Tsinghua University

Principle measures of the graduate education reform of Tsinghua University in 2016.

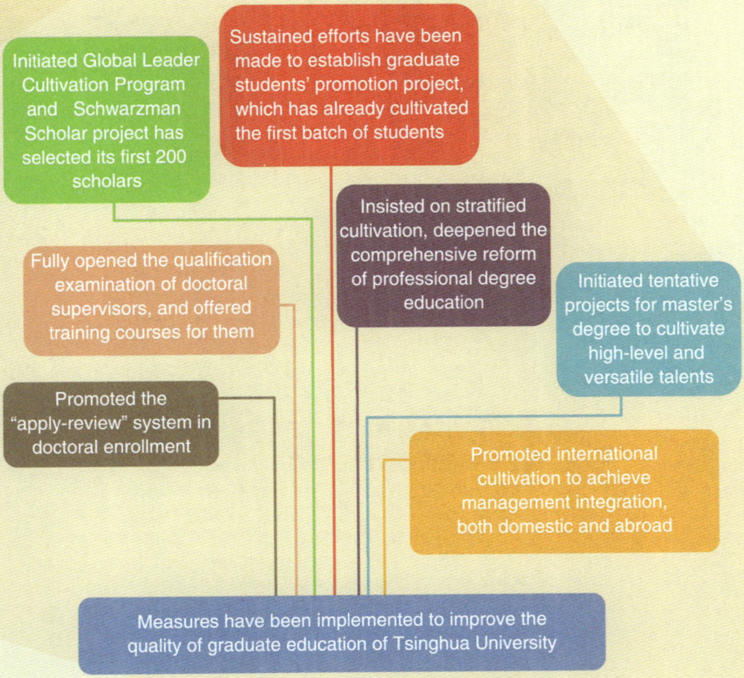

2. 苏州大学研究生教育

2016 年苏州大学研究生教育改革主要举措：

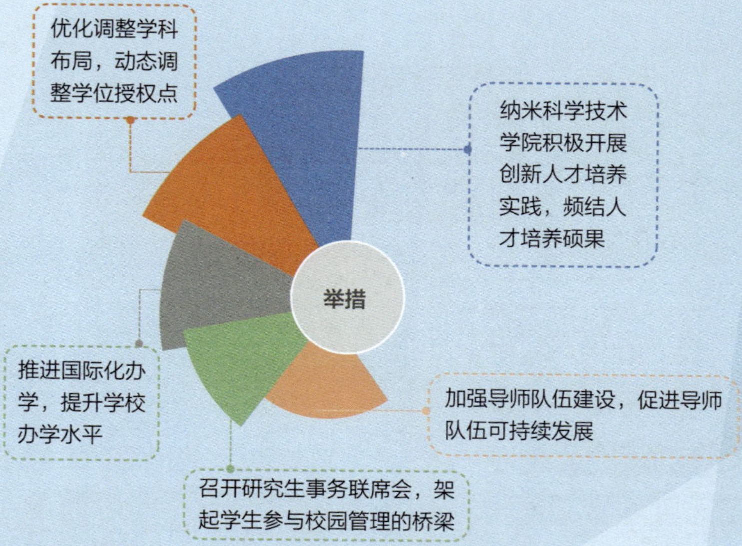

2. Graduate education in Soochow University

Chief Measures of Reform on Graduate Education in 2016.

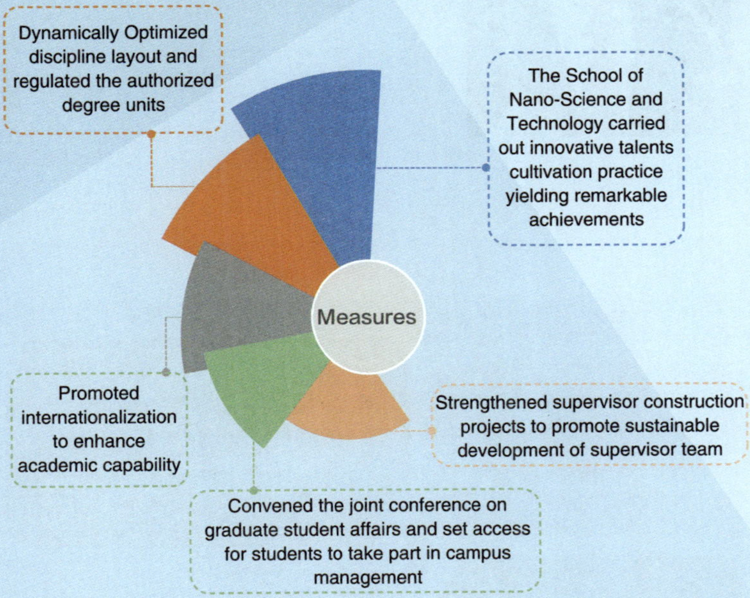

（三）华南理工大学何镜堂院士和他的研究生教育秘籍

何镜堂院士

何镜堂院士长期坚持科研与教学相结合培养建筑学领军人才，至今已培养出近百位研究生。这些学生中，有些已经晋升为教授、院长、总建筑师，成为广东省乃至全国建筑设计和教育领域的主要骨干力量。

秘籍

第一，学建筑首先要学会做人，要有责任感和职业道德

第二，以“两观三性”的创作理念来指导学生，树立起正确的建筑观，不要盲目抄袭或片面追求形式

第三，强调创作思维的培养，抓主要矛盾和矛盾的主要方面，作出正确的判断和设计定位

第四，学会团队合作

III. Academician He Jingtang from South China University of Technology and his personal advice concerning graduate education

He Jingtang, Academician

Academician He Jingtang has insisted on combining the teaching and researching together in training architecture talents for a long time. He has cultivated nearly 100 postgraduates, majority of whom are professors, deans and chief architects, who have served as the backbones in architectural and educational fields of Guangdong province as well as nationwide.

Educational Know-Hows

1. Learn to be the responsible professionals with high ethical standards before learning architecture

2. Guide students with "2 observation points and 3 characters", build the correct architectural notions without plagiarizing or formalizing one-sidedly

3. Emphasize the cultivation of innovative thinking, grasp main contradictions, and strive to make the right judgment and orientation

4. Learn from team work

三、"省"说
研究生教育质量

（一）人才培养大比拼

1. 基础研究谁最强

排名得分第一的为**北京**，它在 2016 年国家社科基金重大项目的申报中获得 65 项资助，在国家自然科学基金的重大项目申报中获得 23 项资助（图 3.1）。

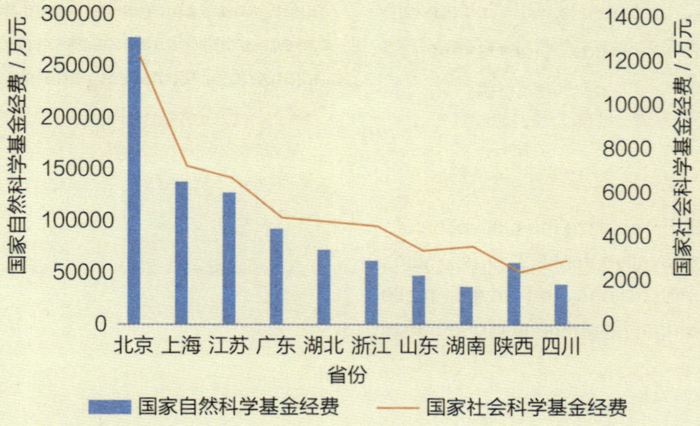

图 3.1　2016 年基金项目获批经费前 10 名的省（市）

Graduate Education Quality in Each Province

I. Competition on Talent Training

1. Who was the most qualified in fundamental researches

In 2016, Beijing ranked first in this field. The city received 65 grants of major projects from the National Social Science Foundation and 23 from the National Natural Science Foundation (Chart 3.1).

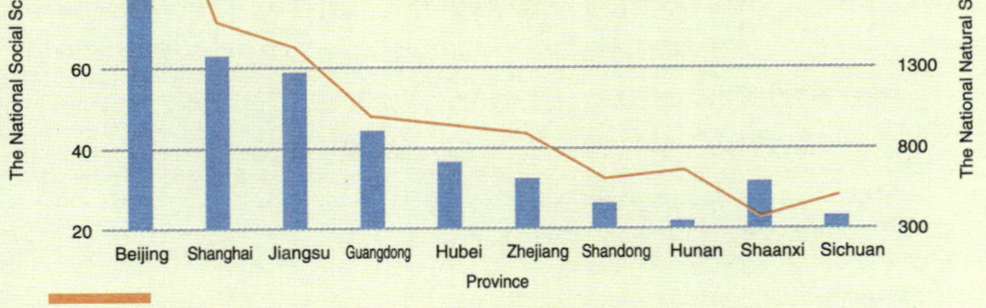

Chart 3.1 Top 10 Funding of Projects in 2016 (by province / city)

2. 学术平台水平排名

按照优秀学科数与一级学科博士点数的比例来考察各省学科平台的质量，**浙江省跃居第一**（表 3.1）。

表 3.1　2016 年省、市学科平台质量前 10 名

省份	排名	优秀学科数		一级学科博士点数
		学位中心	ESI	
浙江	1	30	36	84
上海	2	61	81	214
北京	3	164	123	549
湖北	4	43	51	182
湖南	5	31	31	129
天津	6	20	19	85
广东	7	21	48	141
江苏	8	41	85	281
安徽	9	10	21	75
黑龙江	10	14	22	96

3. 师比排名

研究生生师比最低的前四位为河南、青海、海南和宁夏，生师比均低于 4（图 3.2）。

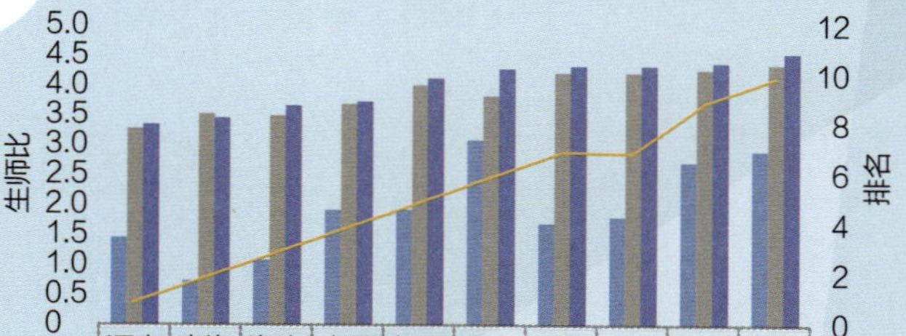

	河南	青海	海南	宁夏	新疆	山东	江西	广西	贵州	河北
博士生师比	1.49	0.77	1.12	1.95	1.96	3.12	1.73	1.84	2.75	2.94
硕士生师比	3.31	3.56	3.53	3.73	4.05	3.87	4.26	4.26	4.31	4.4
研究生生师比	3.38	3.49	3.7	3.77	4.16	4.32	4.37	4.37	4.42	4.58
排名	1	2	3	4	5	6	7	7	9	10

图 3.2　2016 年研究生生师比前 10 名的省（市）

2. Rankings in Academic Platform Quality

We chose the number of excellent disciplines and the first-level disciplines authorized to offer doctorate degree to examine the quality of the provincial academic platform quality. The result shows that Zhejiang province ranked the first on the list (Sheet 3.1).

Sheet 3.1 Top 10 of Academic Platform Quality in 2016 (by province/ city)

Province	Rank	Excellent disciplines		First-level disciplines authorized to offer doctorate degree
		CDGDC	ESI	
Zhejiang	1	30	36	84
Shanghai	2	61	81	214
Beijing	3	164	123	549
Hubei	4	43	51	182
Hunan	5	31	31	129
Tianjin	6	20	19	85
Guangdong	7	21	48	141
Jiangsu	8	41	85	281
Anhui	9	10	21	75
Heilongjiang	10	14	22	96

3. Rankings in Student and Teacher Ratio (S&T ratio)

The lowest student and teacher ratio (S&T ratio) appeared in Henan, Qinghai, Hainan and Ningxia, which was lower than four (Chart 3.2).

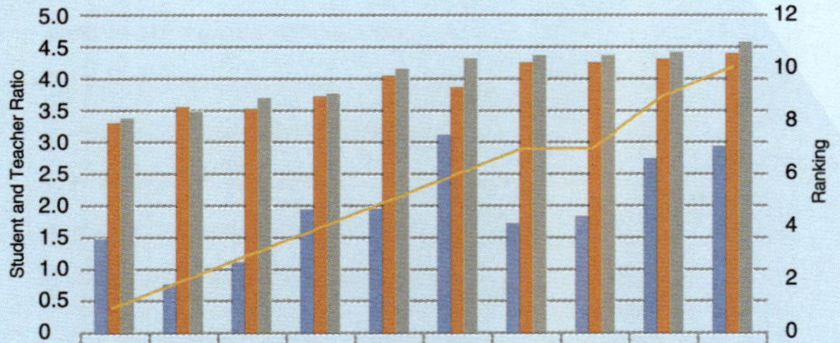

	Henan	Qinghai	Hainan	Ningxia	Xinjiang	Shandong	Jiangxi	Guangxi	Guizhou	Hebei
doctor S&T ratio	1.49	0.77	1.12	1.95	1.96	3.12	1.73	1.84	2.75	2.94
master S&T ratio	3.31	3.56	3.53	3.73	4.05	3.87	4.26	4.26	4.31	4.40
graduate student S&T ratio	3.38	3.49	3.7	3.77	4.16	4.32	4.37	4.37	4.42	4.58
Ranking	1	2	3	4	5	6	7	7	9	10

Chart 3.2 Top 10 of the Student and Teacher Ratio in 2014 (by province/ city)

4. 教研成果排名

从论文发表的情况来看，北京排名第一，其域内学者发表在教育类 CSSCI 期刊上关于研究生教育的学术论文数超过 100 篇（表 3.2）。

表 3.2　2016 年研究生教育规律探索前 10 名的省（市）

省份	排名	研究生教育领域 CSSCI 论文	中国学位与研究生教育优秀成果奖（研究类）			
			第一届		第二届	
			一等奖	二等奖	一等奖	二等奖
北京	1	103	2	1	0	1
江苏	2	54	0	1	0	0
安徽	3	28	0	0	1	0
湖北	4	30	0	0	0	0
湖南	5	20	0	1	0	0
上海	6	29	0	0	0	0
浙江	7	16	0	0	0	0
广东	8	14	0	0	0	0
陕西	9	12	0	0	0	0
山东	10	10	0	0	0	0

5. 国际合作交流水平排名

北京的合作办学项目最多，有 56 个（图 3.3）。此外，有 10 个省份尚未拥有教育部复核通过的中外合作办学项目。

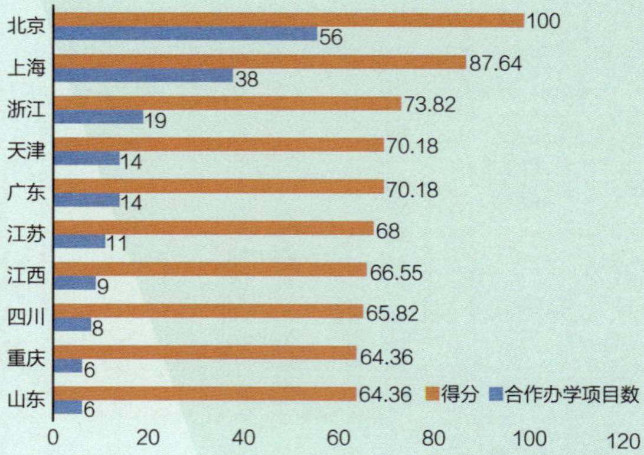

图 3.3　2017 年硕士及以上中外合作办学项目数前 10 名的省（市）

4. Ranking of the teaching and research achievements

For the amount of paper published, Beijing ranked first. The scholars in Beijing published more than 100 academic papers on graduate education in CSSCI journal of the education category (Sheet 3.2).

Sheet 3.2 Top 10 in Exploring the Law of Graduate Education in 2016 (by province/ city)

Province	Rank	CSSCI papers on graduate education	Outstanding Achievement Award in Degree and Graduate Education(Research division)			
			First election		Second election	
			First prize	Second prize	First prize	Second prize
Beijing	1	103	2	1	0	1
Jiangsu	2	54	0	1	0	0
Anhui	3	28	0	0	1	0
Hubei	4	30	0	0	0	0
Hunan	5	20	0	1	0	0
Shanghai	6	29	0	0	0	0
Zhejiang	7	16	0	0	0	0
Guangdong	8	14	0	0	0	0
Shaanxi	9	12	0	0	0	0
Shandong	10	10	0	0	0	0

5. Rankings in international cooperation and exchange

Beijing had the most cooperative education projects, which was up to 56 (Chart 3.3). In addition, 10 provinces didn't have any Sino-foreign running projects or schools approved by the Ministry of Education.

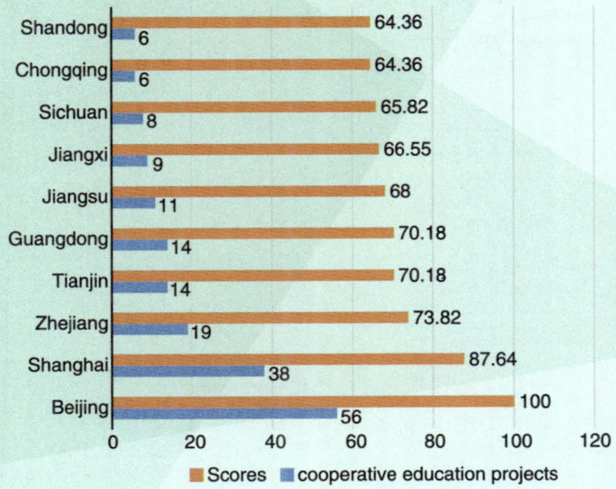

Chart 3.3 Top 10 in the International Cooperation Projects of master's or above (by province/city)

6. 专业学位排名

博士专业学位授权点数量最多的前三名省份分别为**北京、上海**和**江苏**。如西藏、山西和海南等目前暂无博士专业学位授权点。**专业学位硕士点**最多的前三名省市为**北京、江苏**和**湖北**（图3.4）。

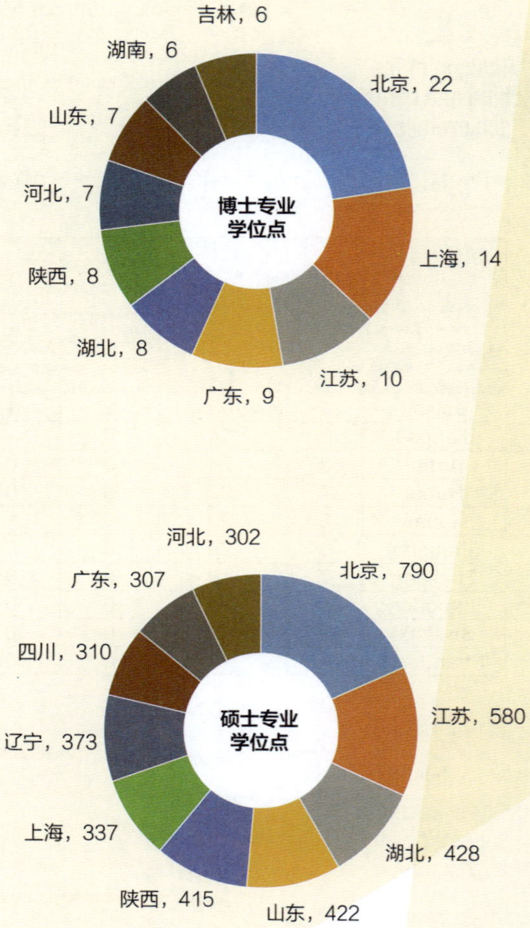

图 3.4　2017 年专业学位点前 10 名的省份

6. Rankings in professional degree

Beijing, Shanghai and Jiangsu were the top three provinces and cities with the most authorized doctoral degree professional programs. However, other provinces such as Tibet, Shanxi and Hainan did not have even one yet. Beijing, Jiangsu and Hubei had the most master's degree professional programs (Chart 3.4).

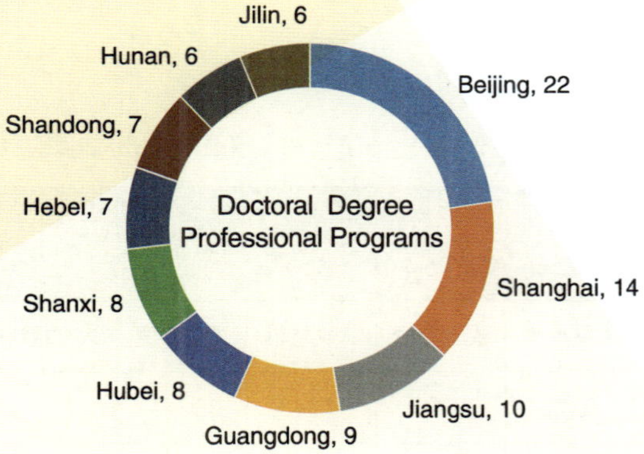

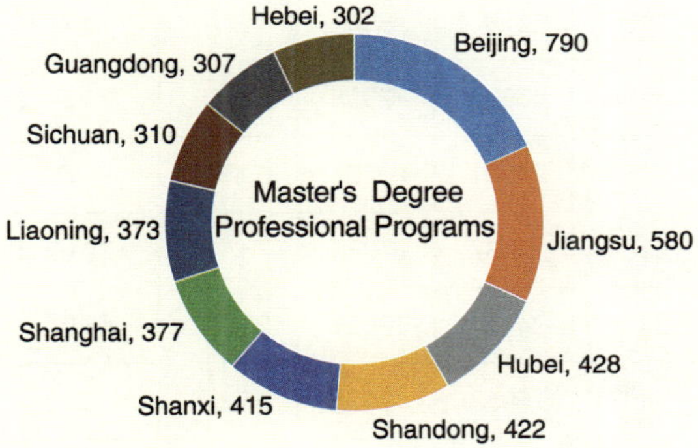

Chart 3.4 Top 10 of Professional Degree Programs in 2017 (by province/city)

（二）教育贡献大比拼

1. 拥有科学研究经历的学术学位研究生人数比例排名

排名第一的**浙江省**，其理工农医的科研参与率高达 **96.24%**，人文社科的科研参与率高达 **27.15%**（表 3.3）。

表 3.3　2015 年学术学位在学研究生拥有科研项目参与经历的比率前 10 名的省份

省份	排名	参与科研的研究生数 / 人		学术学位在学生数 / 人		在学研究生有科研项目参与经历的比率 / %	
		人文社科	理工农医	人文社科	理工农医	人文社科	理工农医
浙江	1	3195	27207	11770	28271	27.15	96.24
宁夏	2	98	2122	1006	1655	9.74	128.22
云南	3	1155	11500	8387	10178	13.77	112.99
天津	4	3156	16629	12358	21345	25.54	77.91
四川	5	5884	26931	20562	39037	28.62	68.99
江苏	6	5966	59887	27083	76776	22.03	78.00
广东	7	2866	34150	19051	35291	15.04	96.77
贵州	8	107	6953	3125	5457	3.42	127.41
青海	9	81	799	926	754	8.75	105.97
湖南	10	2793	20346	16077	26697	17.37	76.21

II. Competition on Education Contribution

1. Rankings regarding the ratio of academic graduate students with scientific research experiences

Zhejiang Province ranked first in this field. 96.24% of the students took part in the research in the fields of Science, Engineering, Agriculture and Medicine, meanwhile, 27.15% of the students in the fields of Humanities and Social Science (Sheet 3.3).

Sheet 3.3 Top 10 in Academic Graduate Students with Scientific Research Experiences in 2015 (by province)

Province	Rank	Graduate students with research experience(A)		Graduate students with academic degree(B)		Ratio of the students with research experience (A/B) / %	
		Humanities and Social Science	Science, Engineering, Agriculture and Medicine	Humanities and Social Science	Science, Engineering, Agriculture and Medicine	Humanities and Social Science	Science, Engineering, Agriculture and Medicine
Zhejiang	1	3195	27207	11770	28271	27.15	96.24
Ningxia	2	98	2122	1006	1655	9.74	128.22
Yunnan	3	1155	11500	8387	10178	13.77	112.99
Tianjin	4	3156	16629	12358	21345	25.54	77.91
Sichuan	5	5884	26931	20562	39037	28.62	68.99
Jiangsu	6	5966	59887	27083	76776	22.03	78.00
Guangdong	7	2866	34150	19051	35291	15.04	96.77
Guizhou	8	107	6953	3125	5457	3.42	127.41
Qinghai	9	81	799	926	754	8.75	105.97
Hunan	10	2793	20346	16077	26697	17.37	76.21

2. 全国性竞赛获奖数排名

从各省（市）获得中国研究生创新实践系列大赛奖励来看，上海稳居第一，遥遥领先（表 3.4）。

表 3.4　2016 年在学研究生获得中国研究生创新实践系列大赛奖励前 10 名的省份

省份	排名	特等奖	一等奖	二等奖	三等奖
上海	1	0	39	547	610
江苏	2	0	30	240	225
北京	3	1	36	133	197
陕西	4	1	27	129	167
湖北	5	0	31	129	123
山东	6	0	10	93	107
浙江	7	0	11	59	75
湖南	8	1	8	59	66
重庆	9	0	7	49	87
四川	10	1	12	41	59

3. 中国学位与研究生教育成果奖（实践类）获奖数排名

北京作为知名高校的聚集地获得了绝大多数的奖励，其中包括一等奖 3 项，二等奖 6 项（图 3.5）。

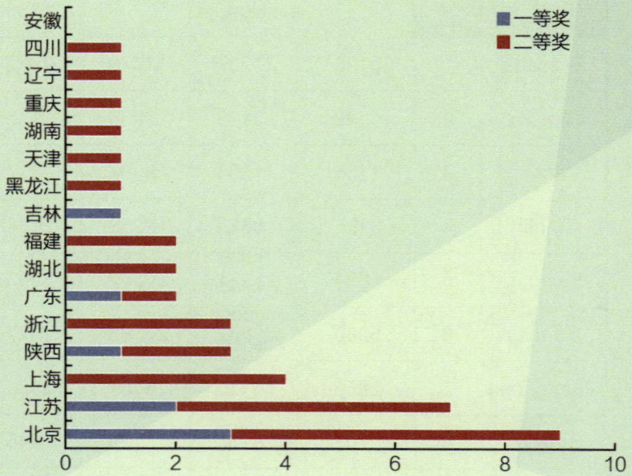

图 3.5　2016 年各省（市）第二届中国学位与研究生教育成果奖（实践类）获奖数

2. Rankings in the number of graduate students winning prizes in national competitions

Shanghai ranked first, far ahead nationwide in the awards from the innovative practice series obtained by the graduate students (Sheet 3.4).

Sheet 3.4 Top 10 of Graduate student Winning Prize in National Completion in 2016 (by province/city)

Province	Rank	Grand Prize	First Prize	Second Prize	Third Prize
Shanghai	1	0	39	547	610
Jiangsu	2	0	30	240	225
Beijing	3	1	36	133	197
Shaanxi	4	1	27	129	167
Hubei	5	0	31	129	123
Shandong	6	0	10	93	107
Zhejiang	7	0	11	59	75
Hunan	8	1	8	59	66
Chongqing	9	0	7	49	87
Sichuan	10	1	12	41	59

3. Rankings in the outstanding achievement award (education practice division) in graduate education

Beijing, as the gathering place of well-known universities obtained most of the awards, including 3 first prizes, and 6 second prizes (Chart 3.5).

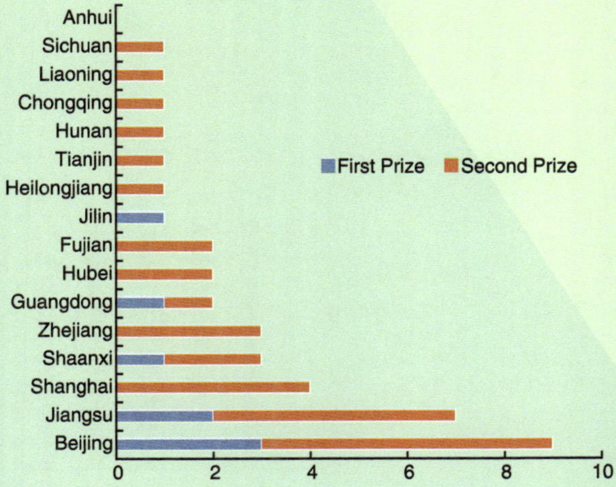

Chart 3.5 Outstanding Achievement Awards (Education practice division) in 2016 (by province/city)

（三）社会贡献大比拼

1. 经济贡献度排名

上海、河南、广西、江西、广东和宁夏近 5 年研究生招生规模的变化与其 GDP 的变化呈现正向的中、高度相关，说明这些省份研究生的招生较好地考虑了 GDP 变化所表征的经济发展需求变化（图 3.6）。

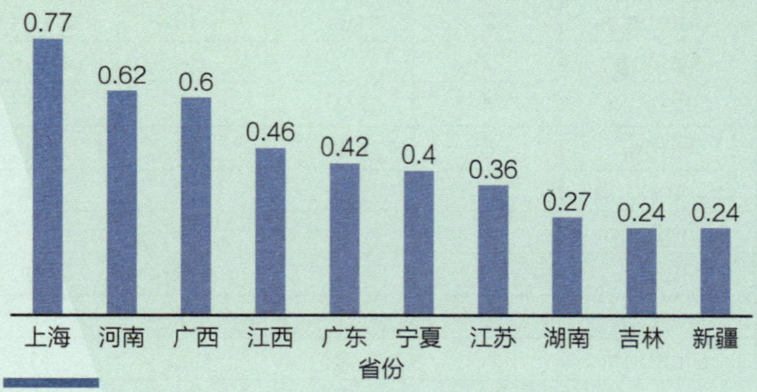

图 3.6　分省（市）研究生招生规模增量与 GDP 增量的相关系数（2011—2015）

2. 科技贡献度排名

宁夏、北京和重庆近 5 年研究生招生规模的变化与其技术市场成交额增量的变化呈现正向的高度相关（图 3.7）。

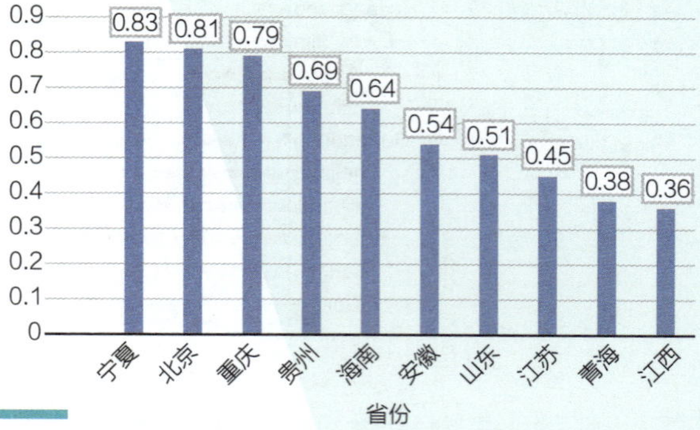

图 3.7　分省（市）研究生招生规模增量与技术市场成交额增量的相关系数（2011—2015）

III. Competition on Social contribution

1. Economic contribution rate rankings

In the last five years, the changes in the enrollment scale of graduate students in Shanghai, Henan, Guangxi, Jiangxi, Guangdong and Ningxia were positively correlated with their GDP changes. This means that the enrollment of the graduates in these provinces was well taken into account in the needs of the economic development, which was characterized by GDP changes (Chart 3.6).

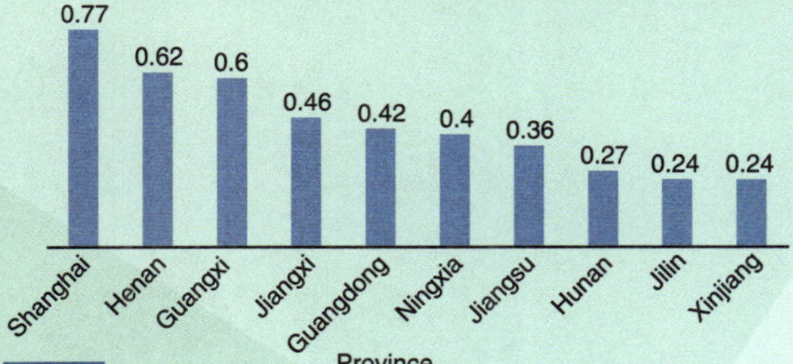

Chart 3.6 Correlation Coefficient of the Increase in Enrollment of the Graduates and GDP from 2011 to 2015 (by province/city)

2. Science and technology contribution rate rankings

In the last five years, the changes in the enrollment scale of graduate students in Ningxia, Beijing and Chongqing were positively correlated with the changes in the volume of the technology market (Chart 3.7).

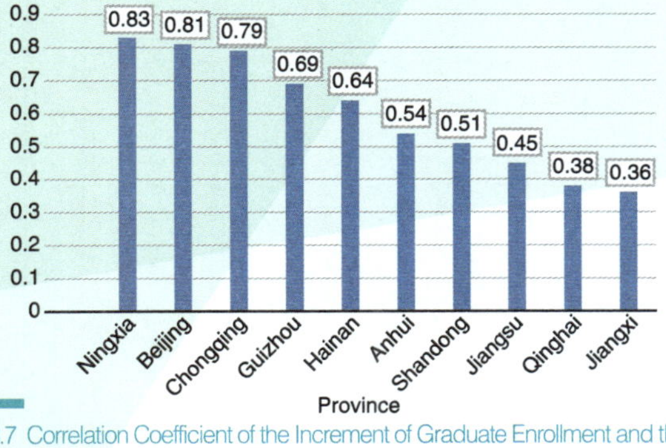

Chart 3.7 Correlation Coefficient of the Increment of Graduate Enrollment and the Increase of volume of technology Market (2011—2015) (by province/city)

3. 就业贡献度排名

北京、上海、天津是研究生“密度”最大的三个城市，就业人口中具有研究生学历人数的占比分别为**6.1%**，**4.8%**和**2.3%**。

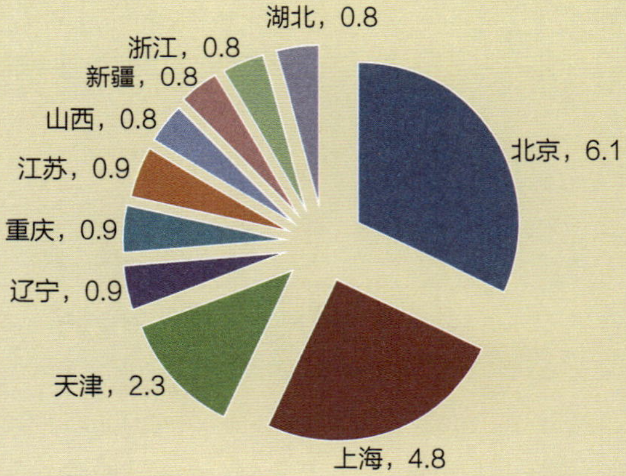

3. Employment contribution rate rankings

Beijing, Shanghai and Tianjin were the top three cities which had the highest population density with graduate degrees. Employees with graduate degree accounted for 6.1%, 4.8% and 2.3% respectively.

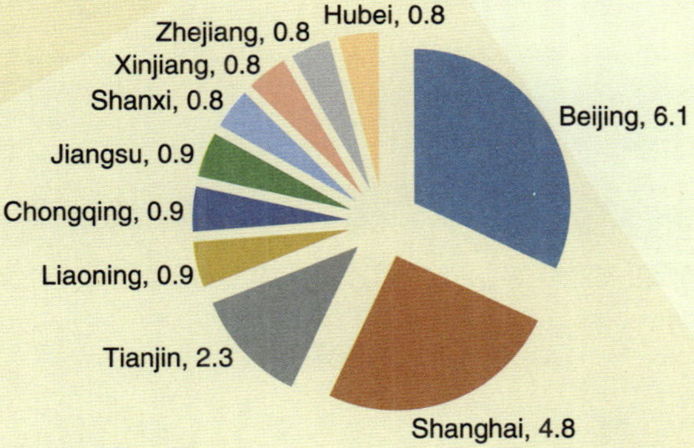

四、"生"说
研究生教育质量

（一）"我们"来评研究生培养质量

2017 年，我们共调查了 109 个研究生培养单位，其中"985 工程"高校 26 所，"211 工程"高校 29 所，其他高校 53 所，科研院所 1 所。调查样本分布如下。

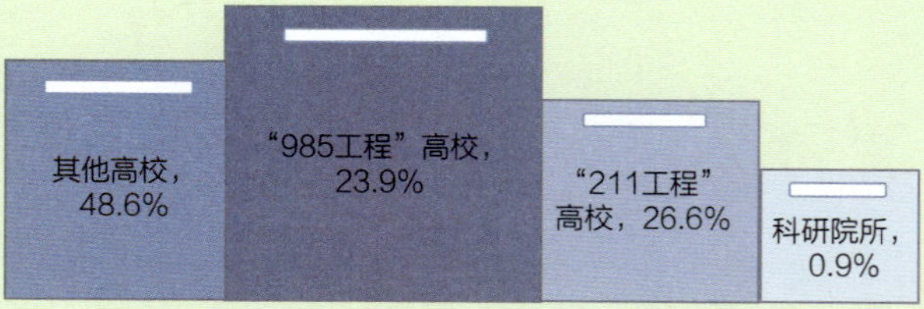

调查对象按性别分：

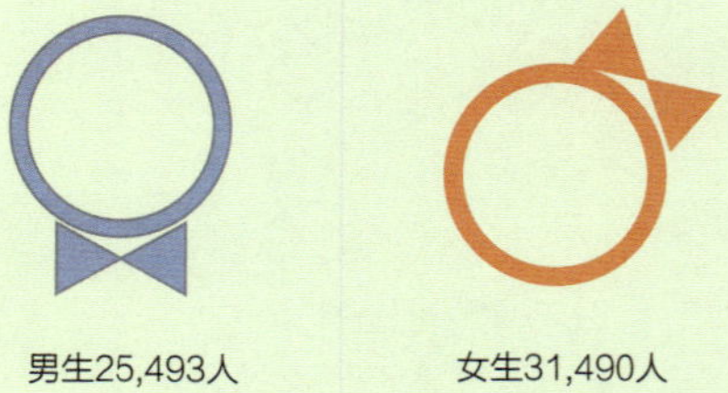

Graduate Education Quality from Students' Perspective

I. Competition on Talent Training

The 2017 survey totally covered 109 graduate training units, including 26 "985 Project" universities, 29 "211 Project" universities, 53 other universities and 1 research institutions. Sampling distribution is in the chart.

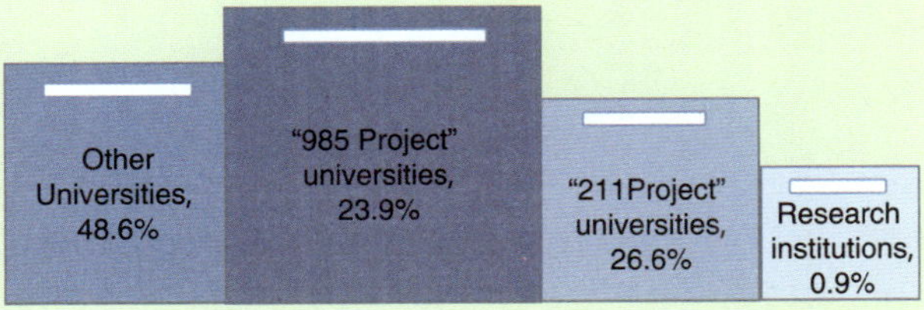

By Gender

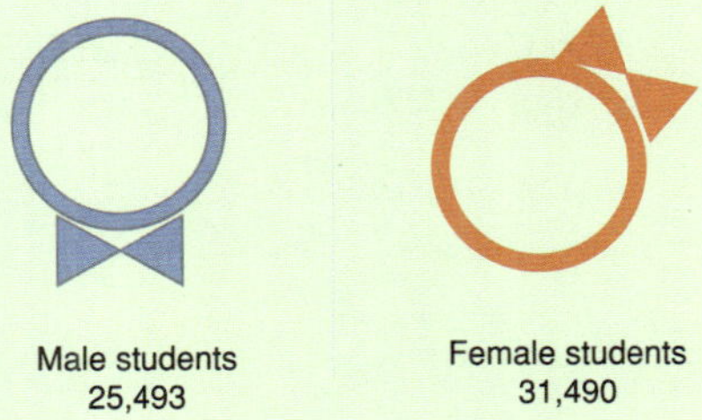

按培养层次分：

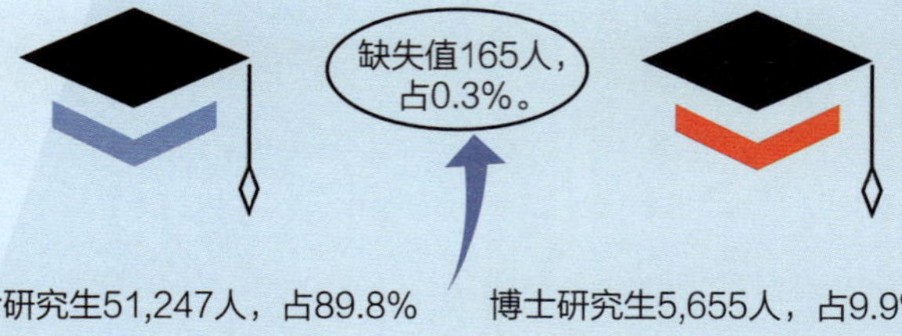

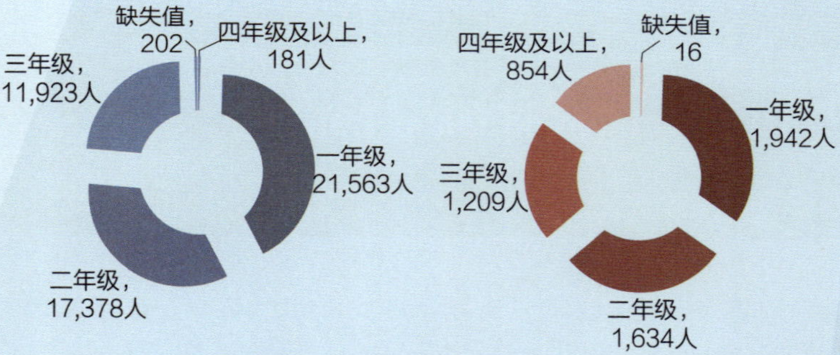

按培养类型分：

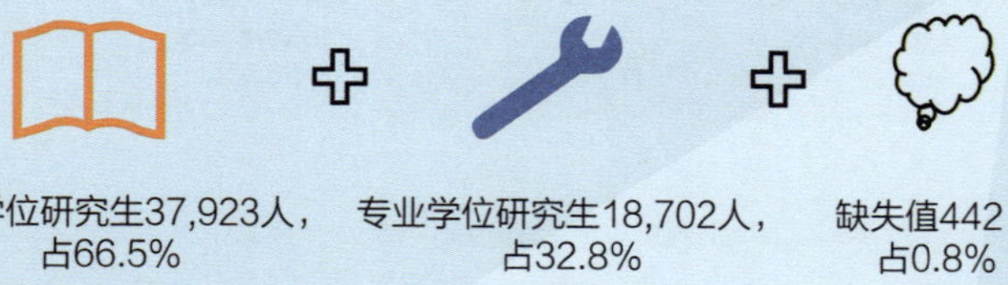

By Degree

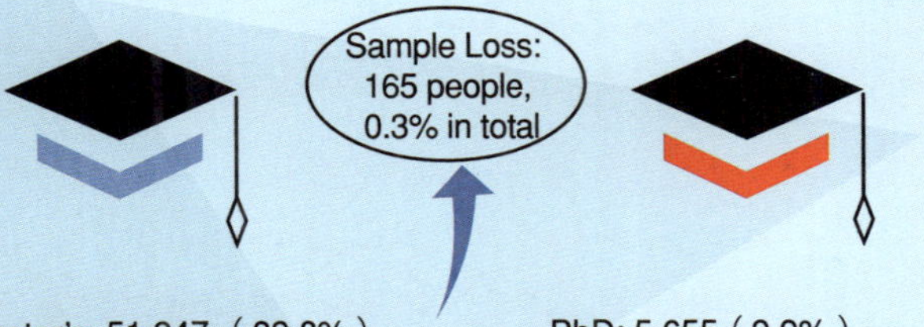

Master's: 51,247 (89.8%)

PhD: 5,655 (9.9%)

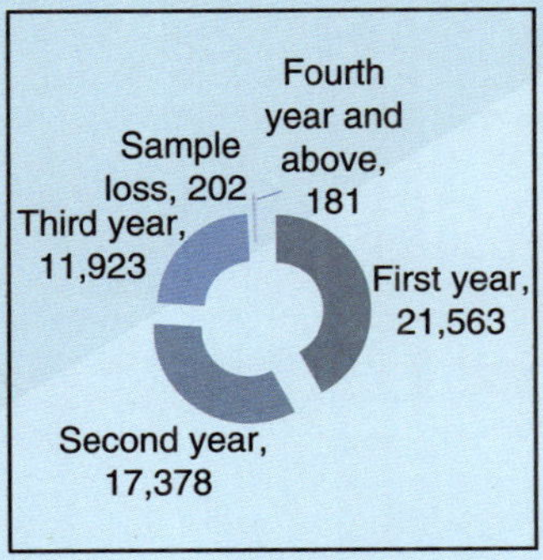

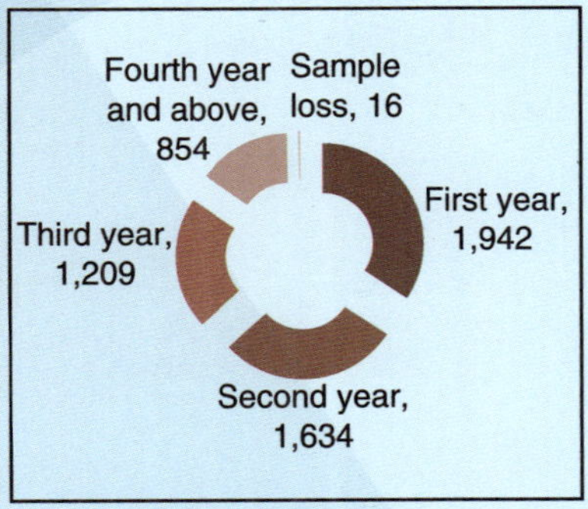

By Training Style

Academic Degree Students, 37,923 (66.5%)

Professional Degree students, 18,702 (32.8%)

Sample Loss, 442 (0.8%)

（二）“我们”对研究生培养质量满意吗

1. 研究生总体满意度

研究生对研究生教育的总体满意率达到 70.6%

（1）不同性别群体，男女生对研究生教育的总体满意率为：

71.0%　　70.2 %

（2）各类培养单位中，对研究生教育的总体满意度分别为：

“985工程”高校研究生	“211工程”高校研究生	科研院所	其他高校研究生
72.1%	69.5%	69.5%	69.0%

II. Is the Graduate Education Quality Satisfying

1. Overall satisfaction of graduate students

The overall satisfaction rate from students undergoing graduate education was 70.6%

A. Satisfaction Rate by Gender

71.0%

70.2 %

B. Satisfaction Rate by Institution

"985 Project" universities	"211 Project" universities	Research institutions	Other Universities
72.1%	69.5%	69.5%	69.0%

（3）在各学科门类学术学位研究生中，哲学研究生的总体满意度最高，满意率达到 77.0%（图 4.1）。

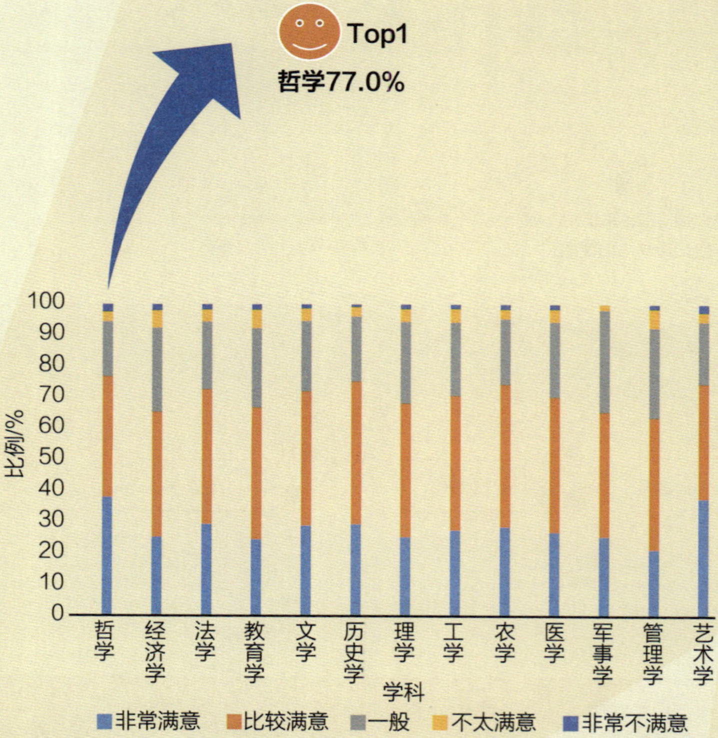

图 4.1　各学科总体满意度

（4）博士生的总体满意度高于硕士生。博士生的总体满意率达 73.3%，硕士研究生总体满意率为 70.3%。

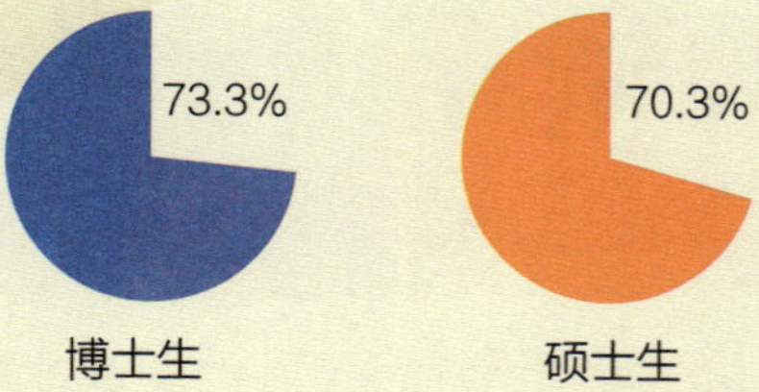

C. Among the respondents, students in philosophy had the highest satisfaction rate, which had reached 77.0% (Chart 4.1).

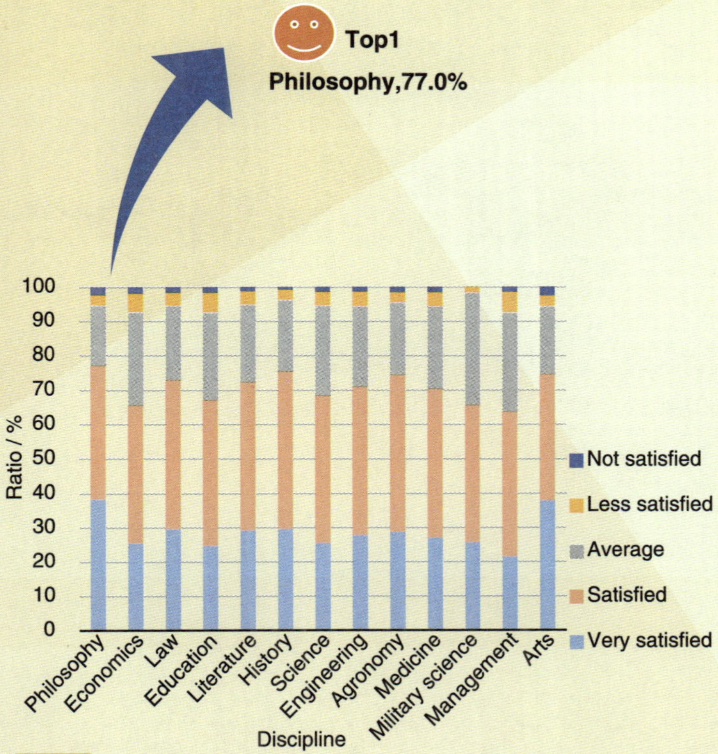

Chart 4.1 Satisfaction Rate by Disciplines

D. Doctoral students had a higher satisfaction rate than the master's, which is 73.3% compared to 70.3%.

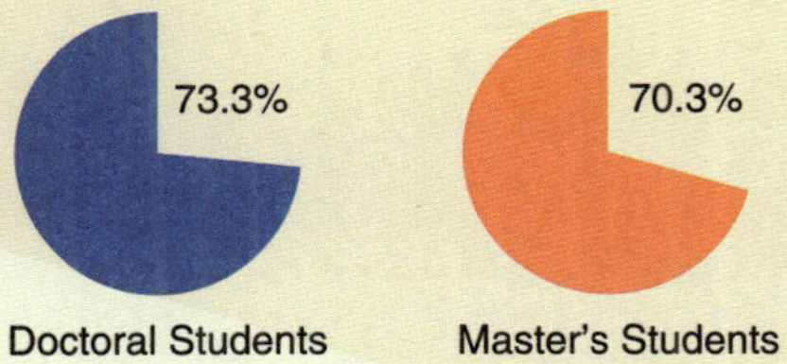

2. 课程教学满意度

研究生对课程教学的满意率为 69.4%。

在各类培养单位中，最高与最低满意率分属“985 工程”高校和“211 工程”高校。

3. 科研训练满意度

研究生对科研训练的满意率为：

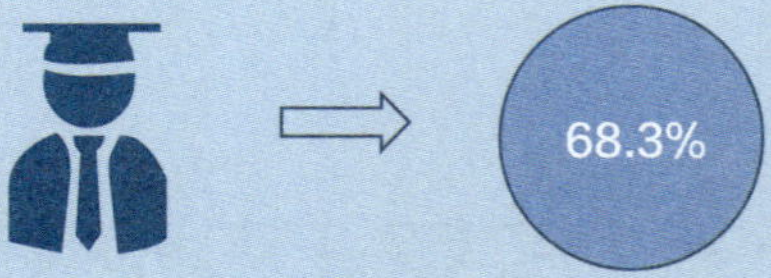

（1）在各类培养单位中，科研院所研究生对科研训练的满意度最高，满意率达到了 76.1%，“211 工程”高校研究生对科研训练的满意度最低，仅为 65.5%。

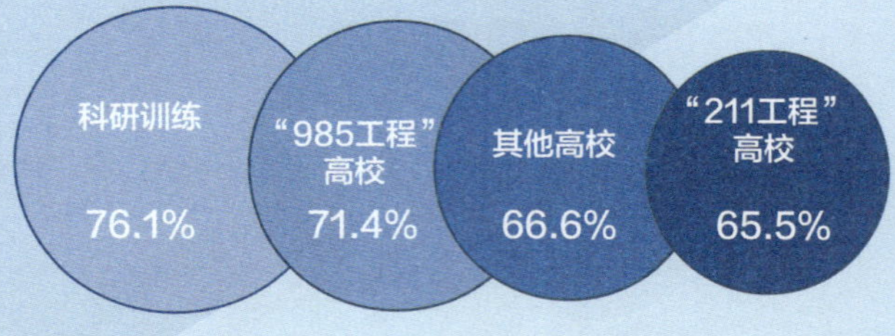

2. Satisfaction for curriculum

The graduate students' satisfaction rate for curriculum was 69.4%.

Among all the institutions, the highest and the lowest satisfaction rate belonged to "985" project universities and "211" project universities separately.

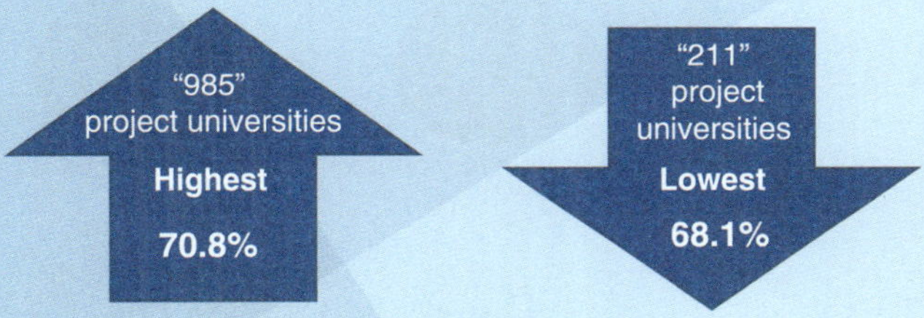

3. Satisfaction for research training

Graduate students' satisfaction rate for research training was 68.3%.

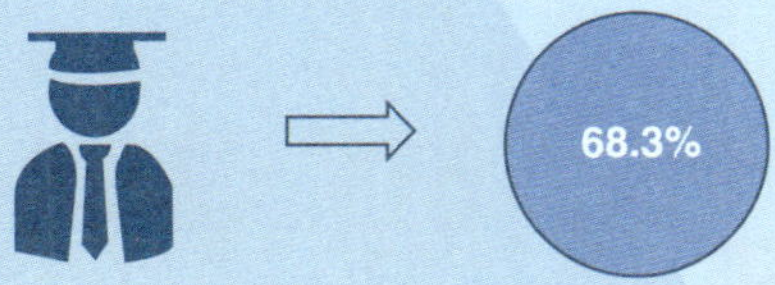

A. In all institutions, graduate students in research institutions had the highest satisfaction rate of 76.1%, while "211" project universities had the lowest, 65.5%.

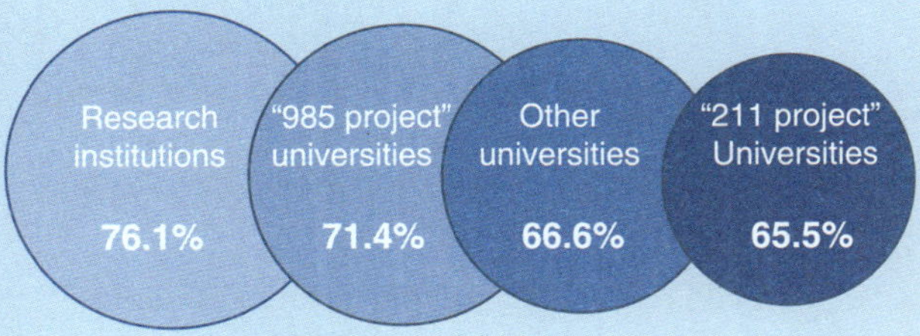

（2）就培养层次而言：

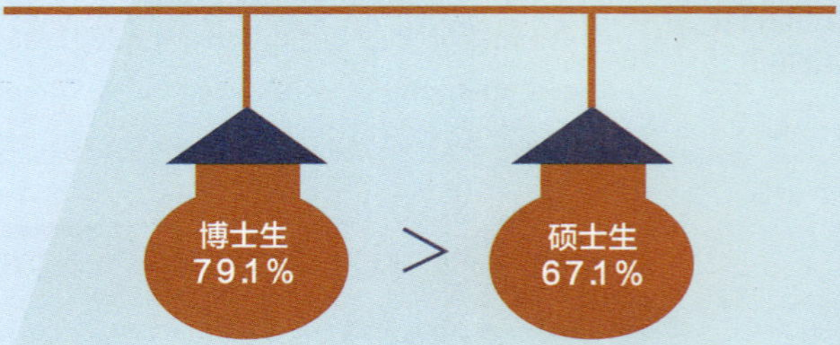

4. 导师满意度

研究生对指导教师的满意率为：

5. 专业学位研究生满意度

专业学位研究生对研究生教育的总体满意度高于学术学位研究生。

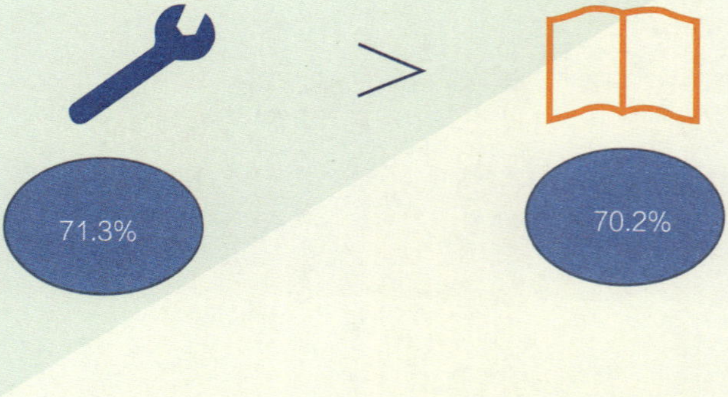

B. By Degree

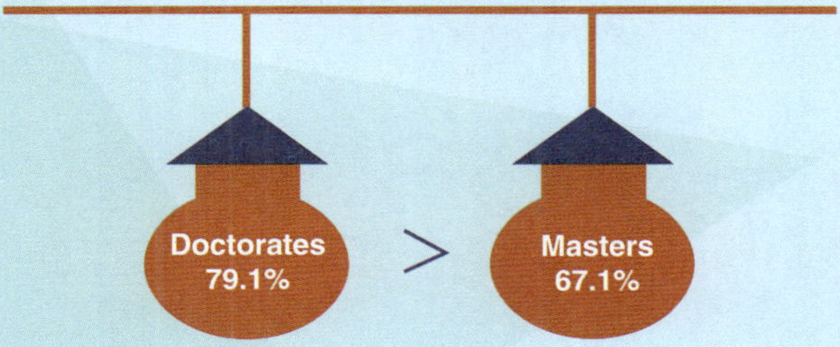

4. Satisfaction for supervisors

The satisfaction rate for supervisors was 68.3%.

5. Satisfaction from professional graduate students

Graduate students pursuing professional degrees had higher overall satisfaction rate on graduate education compared the students for academic degrees.

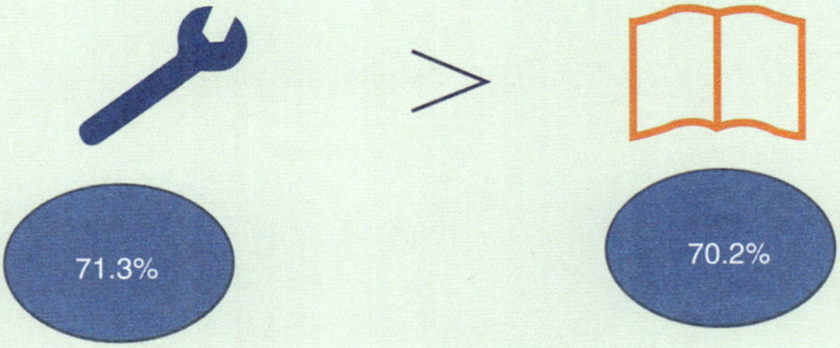

五、“他”说研究生教育质量

（一）国外媒体评价中国研究生教育，那么问题来了

1. 通过 20 年来的努力，中国高校是否能跻身世界一流大学名单

2. 中国的世界一流大学建设需要方向

International Reviews of Graduate Education

I. China's Graduate Education in the Eyes of Foreign Medias

1. Through 20 years of efforts, could Chinese universities list in the top ones in the world

2. China should set a vision for world-class universities

（二）厉害了？亚洲国家研究生教育质量

01 日本：提议“卓越研究生院”事业，强化国际竞争力

02 韩国：研究生未为职业生涯做好充分准备

03 印度：政府设立国家博士后奖学金，资助“纯科学研究”的博士后学业

04 马来西亚：高等教育部将创建博士学位登记制度

II. Graduate Education Quality in Other Asian Countries

01 Japan: proposed "excellence graduate school" plan to strengthen international competitiveness

02 Korean: graduate students not fully prepared for career

03 India: the government set up the national postdoctoral scholarship to fund the pure scientific research for the postdoctoral education

04 Malaysia: The Ministry of Higher Education would create a doctoral degree registration system

（三）世界这么大，国外研究生教育动态先让你看看

III. How is the Graduate Education Going in Foreign Countries

01 Improvement and development of online degree programs

02 Brexit would bring serious impact on British universities

03 Funding sources and subsidies of higher education

A. One of the German universities revised the dispute funding agreement

B. Canada: large universities were more likely to receive research funds

C. Brazil: scientists fought for the funding freezing in the next 20 years

04 The surge in the number of doctoral students in Denmark had no negative impact on its quality of doctoral education

05 Russia released "5-100" Plan to build high-level universities

06 Study concerning the cognition of graduate education from the view of university academics

后 记

《五说中国研究生教育质量（2017）》中英文版本，是《六说中国研究生教育质量》的年度升级版。本报告通过运用大量数据，以简单、明了、直观的图表等表达方式，以“五说”：数说、事说、省说、生说、他说为编排顺序，运用大量图表，直观表现了 2016 年度我国研究生教育质量状况。报告使用简洁活泼、通俗易懂、贴近生活的语言，使广大读者能够轻松读懂本报告。本报告大体呈现了 2016 年度我国研究生教育质量状态，如读者需要详细、全面了解 2016 年度我国研究教育质量状态，还需阅读《中国研究生教育质量年度报告（2017）》。

本报告的编写和出版，是中国研究生教育质量编研组集体劳动的结晶。在此，首先要感谢编研组全体成员的辛勤劳作和付出。本报告由荣利颖、娄枝、杨旭婷负责翻译，高珊负责审校工作。课题组秘书组织筹划了本报告的编辑工作。同时，中国科学技术出版社王晓义主任为本报告的策划、出版和发行等付出了大量的努力和辛劳，在此表示非常感谢。

《五说中国研究生教育质量（2017）》是编研组继《六说中国研究生教育质量》之后的又一次尝试，肯定存在不足，恳请读者指正。同时，在今后工作中也会不断改进本报告及《中国研究生教育质量年度报告（2017）》的编研水平，为广大读者服务，为推动我国研究生教育质量的提高服务。

王战军
2017 年 7 月于北京

Postscript

The *China's Graduate Education Quality Data on Five Aspects 2017* is an upgraded version based on the *China's Graduate Education Quality Data on Six Aspects*. The report illustrated China's graduate education quality in 2016 intuitively from numerical, narrative, provincial, graduate and oversea aspects by using a great amount of data and concise charts. The report adopted popular and lively language, which made it easier for readers to understand, and demonstrated the quality of Chinese graduate education in 2016 generally. Readers could choose the *Annual Report on China's Graduate Education Quality 2017* to get a deeper understanding.

The compilation and publishing of the book is owing to the teamwork of China's graduate education quality research group. Thanks to all the members of the research group for their hard work and dedication. Besides, Rong Liying, Lou Zhi and Yang Xuting helped the translation, Gao Shan helped the review, and the secretary of research group helped the organization. Meanwhile, Director Wang Xiaoyi from China Science and Technology Press made great contribution for the planning, publishing and releasing of the report.

The *China's Graduate Education Quality Data on Five Aspects 2017* is another try after 2016. It could not be faultless and your comments would be highly appreciated. We will continue to improve the report and strengthen our research in the future work to provide better service for the readers and the development of China's graduate education quality.

Wang Zhanjun

2017.07, Beijing